Be a Model Communicator
and Sell your Models to Anyone

Peter L. Bonate, PhD
Astellas Pharma
Senior Director, Pharmacokinetics, Modeling, & Simulation
Northbrook, Illinois

Be a Model Communicator and Sell your Models to Anyone

By Peter L. Bonate, PhD

Copyright © 2014 by Peter L. Bonate

Printed in the United States

ISBN: 978-0-692-32381-6

Contents

Preface

I never paid much attention to public speaking until a few years ago. For the longest time I thought I was a great public speaker. When speaking in front of groups, I wasn't all that nervous; there was some nervousness, but not overwhelmingly so. I wasn't afraid of failure or that people would laugh at me. It was part of my job and I did it. At no time did I seek to become a better speaker, to look for where I might be failing, or to see where I could improve.

It wasn't until after I finished my doctorate degree and was out of school for a few years that I began to take an interest in public speaking. I had a public speaking disaster. The irony, though, was that I didn't realize it was a disaster at all. I thought everything was just fine. It started when I was invited to speak at the Food and Drug Administration (FDA) about how I was analyzing data from electrocardiograms (ECGs) to determine whether a drug was adversely prolonging the repolarization time of the heart. I was thrilled. This was a big deal. Not everyone is invited to speak at the FDA. My talk went well enough. No controversies. I went home feeling ecstatic about my accomplishment.

A film company was at the meeting, videotaping the entire event, and broadcasting it across the country. Before I left Washington, DC, I asked the company to send me a videotape of my presentation. My mother was coming to visit and I wanted to show off to her. Look what your big-shot son did. Just before my mother came to visit, I decided to watch the tape. I grabbed a beer, sat down, and waited to be awed by my awesomeness. Within minutes I was horrified. Every, uh, other, uh, word, uh, out, uh, of my mouth, uh, was "Uh!" It was a freak show. I was so embarrassed by my ineptitude that I turned it off. I didn't show it to my mother. In fact, to this day, I've never shown it to anyone. This event was the turning point of my interest in communication and public speaking. It is also what convinced me of the importance in learning how to be a "model communicator."

Over the years, I've read dozens of books on giving presentations and on how to present scientific data. As far as I am aware, no book has been written with modelers in mind and only a few are written for scientists, in general. Yet I tried to learn what I could from them. I've learned that it's not just about the content of your material. There is a whole other side to presentations--beyond the data--that relates to you and how you are perceived by the audience, how you present, and how you connect. This is the human side of presenting. I decided that a book needed to be written about this because most modelers focus entirely on the presentation. The presentation is only part of the story. You are the other part and that part has been ignored for too long.

I've written other books, technical ones on modeling, simulation, and statistics. One could say they were dry. Scientific. I wanted this one to be different. I wanted this one to be fun and conversational in a sense, with me doing all the talking. I wanted someone who read this book to really have fun with it. By keeping it light and easy to read I hope its message will be clearly heard: not only do you need to present your results clearly and concisely to your audience, you need to sell yourself, the model, and the results. I also hope you enjoy this book and have as much fun reading it as I had writing it.

One thing I would like to ask is that if you have a particular success story, an epic fail, or you feel that you have a great example of model communication please share it with me. I think that what I have written scratches the surface of what I could have written and that sometime in the future I will write a second edition. I would like to be able to put more real-life examples and stories in the next edition. So if you feel like sharing with me, please email me at peter.bonate@gmail.com. Thank you.

There are many people I'd like to thank who were helpful to me in writing this book. I'd like to thank the reviewers for their thoughtful comments: Don Berk, Robert Bies, Christiane Collins, Dan Howard, Vijay Ivaturi, Stacey Tannenbaum, and Jan-Stefan van der Walt. I would like to thank Stephanie Clarke of Clarke International Writing Services for her helpful editorial comments. I would also like to thank all those who allowed me to reprint their photos or illustrations: Kalid Azad, Linda Booth-Sweeney, Dean Bottino, The Jimmy Carter Library and Museum, Holly Chaffin, Conde Nast, King Features Syndicate, Antonio Marques, Kate McCurrach, The Estate of Pablo Picasso, and Wikimedia Commons.

Lastly, I want thank my wife Diana, who always encourages me in these Quixotic book-writing endeavors. She is the love of my life and I am lucky to have her.

Peter Bonate
September 2014

– One–
Introduction

"I, um, analyzed the data from clinical study 001-003. There were, let me see, 1,322 patients, 625 were male and, um, 697 females. The average age was 54.22 years with a range of 18 to 78 years and, um, a median of 55.5 years. Of these, 1,175 had Type II diabetes and, um, 45 had Type I diabetes (pause). You'll notice that the number of Type I and Type II diabetics don't add up to 1,322. We had two sites that did not indicate what type of diabetes the patients had when they enrolled in the study. We tried to contact them and follow-up to determine what type of diabetes the patients had but we were never able to. That leaves, uh, 102 patients that we weren't sure what their illness was."

Bored yet? I am, and I'm writing it. This scientist is supposed to be reporting on the results of an analysis of a clinical study. He's just started his talk and has already fallen off point. He is so far in the woods, even Little Red Riding Hood couldn't find him. His analysis showed that females were 3-times more likely than males to develop cardiac myopathy, a deterioration of the heart wall that can lead to heart failure. Fifteen minutes into the presentation he finally gets to the point. By then, he's lost his audience. Between all the "um's" and "let me see's", he's not exactly the most credible presenter. He seems almost uncertain of his own results. These are important results, but his presentation is so poor that by the time he gets to the point, most of the people in the room aren't paying a whole lot of attention. Then they wake up and, if he's lucky, they'll say "What was that?", "Go over that again, what you just said."

Instead of his way of presenting, how about presenting it like this: Right off the bat, he says "My analysis showed that females were three times more likely than males to develop cardiac myopathy. Given the uncertainty in the data, this value can range from 2.3 to 3.7 times with 95% certainty." This is sure to get the group's attention. Then he says "Now, let me show you how I came to my conclusion." At this point, he proceeds to discuss his methods and other important results.

Notice the difference? It's huge. In both case studies, the presenter is telling the team there was a difference between males and females, but in the first example the presenter took too long to get there and when he finally did, his audience wasn't paying attention. In the second, the point was made up-front with no um's, pauses, or let me see's. There was certainty in the presentation. The audience knows what is coming.

Personally, in my 20 years as a mathematical modeler I would like to say I've had great success throughout my career in the practical application of the models I have developed and in convincing others to use my models. I think I have better success today than when I first started. Early in my career I think, like most modelers, I focused on the technical aspects of my models. How did my residuals look? Was there any model bias? If I used a different estimation algorithm did I get similar parameter estimates? During the model development process I would inevitably fall in love with my models. I know, you should never fall in love with your models, but I couldn't help it. That a few equations could explain all this data made me feel like a brilliant cryptographer who had just cracked some top secret code. When I finished my analysis, I would quickly pull together some slides and present the results to other members of the research team, many of whom were non-modelers, I was stunned when they didn't see what I saw. It was like the team never quite bought into the model and didn't believe the results. Occasionally, somebody would stab a dagger through my heart and say something like "It's only a model," or even worse, "all models are wrong anyway." It was so frustrating. "Can't you see how beautiful this model is? Look at those residuals!" I would want to yell. In the end, I would leave feeling dejected, as if I did all this work for nothing.

Developing a model is not an easy task. Equally difficult, and underappreciated in terms of its impact, is how these models are presented to others. While many in academia may have the funds to develop models through grants that are peer-reviewed, in industry models often have to undergo review by multidisciplinary teams who are not knowledgeable in the nuances of statistical analysis, modeling, or simulation. For instance, in drug development, which is my area of expertise, the project team may consist of a project manager, a statistician, a toxicologist, a variety of physicians, a medical writer, and a regulatory affairs professional. Of these, the statistician is the most quantitative in how they think.

In presenting a model to a project team, the modeler must not only be able to speak to other modelers that might be in the room, but also to any non-scientists that may be in the room. This is what I failed to appreciate early in my career. Rightly or wrongly, the acceptance of a model depends on acceptance from everyone in the room or from some key decision maker, neither of which may have experience in developing or evaluating models.

Then there are times when models are presented to larger audiences where the modeler may not know everyone in the room. This may be at a national meeting or conference, for example. How the model is presented to these two groups will be different. In the smaller project team setting the dynamics are more personal, the presentation is less technical. In the larger group, the dynamics are less intimate and the model is presented in detail. Learning how much detail to present and how to present can mean the difference between acceptance and rejection of a model.

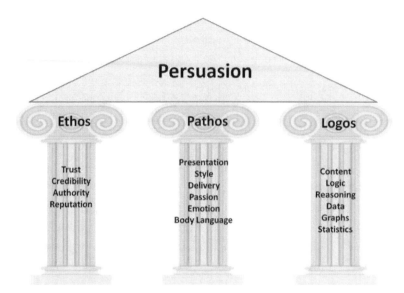

Figure 1. Ethos, Pathos, and Logos are not the names of The Three Musketeers, but instead refer to Aristotle's Pillars of Persuasive Public Speaking, which have formed the basis for convincing and compelling public speaking for over 2,000 years.

More than 2,000 years ago, Aristotle presented the secrets to persuasive public speaking, which he defined as Ethos, Pathos, and Logos (Figure 1). Those secrets still stand today. Some call them the Pillars of Public Speaking and every book on public speaking, this book included, uses these pillars as their foundation. Aristotle defined these as:

- **Ethos** (Greek for "character" or "morals") speaks to the credibility of you as a speaker. Does the audience believe you? Do they respect you? Do you appear trustworthy? Are you an expert on what you are speaking about? Ethos is frequently conveyed by the speaker's reputation. It isn't enough for you to know you are an expert, you have to show your audience that you are the expert.

- **Pathos** (Greek for "suffering" or "experience") speaks to the emotional connection formed between you, as the speaker, and the audience. Is your presentation dynamic or boring? What do your results say and how do they impact the people in the room? Are your results potentially explosive with regards to their conclusions? Pathos is conveyed through emotional and vivid language with the goal of making the audience receptive to your ideas. While certainly the most underappreciated, one may argue that Pathos is the most important of the pillars because an unreceptive audience is an uninterested audience.

- **Logos** (Greek for "word" or "thought") speaks to the logical arguments used to support the main points. As scientists, we are trained to focus on logos. Some scientists focus exclusively on logos. What is the most logical argument we can make? What is the most lucid path from Point A to Point B? The problem is that focusing exclusively on logos ignores the other two pillars. Decisions are rarely made based solely on logic, unless you are Mr. Spock from *Star Trek*. The credibility of the speaker and the relationship they have with the audience are equally important.

In many fields, modelers have had great success in model implementation and usage. Models are used to influence policy decisions, to challenge prevailing theories, to answer difficult questions, and to discover new questions. However, getting to the point of usage can be hard. I work in biology, a field not known for its mathematical rigor. Imagine you have to explain your systems pharmacology model of calcium homeostasis and bone remodeling, which is shown in Figure 2, to a group of physicians, toxicologists, statisticians, and other nontechnical professionals. This is a very complicated model, but it has the useful property of being able to predict long-term changes in bone physiology from short term changes in bone biomarkers, which if measured experimentally could take years of observation. This model can have huge implications for drug development because it means that drug companies may not need long, expensive clinical trials to see if they have an effective drug. They may be able to determine if the drug is effective based on the results of a shorter, less expensive trial focusing on changes in biomarkers. First though, you have to get your team to understand it, and therein lies the heart of the challenge.

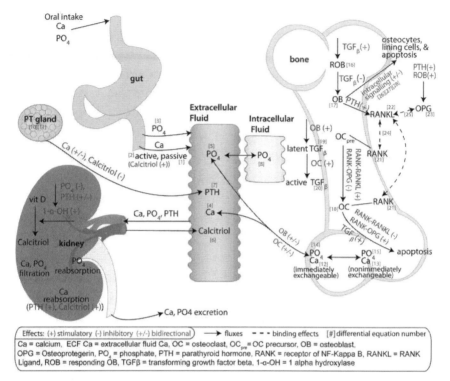

Figure 2. Schematic of a systems pharmacology model used to describe calcium homeostasis and bone remodeling. *Reprinted from M.C. Peterson and M.M. Riggs. A physiologically based mathematical model of integrated calcium homeostasis and bone remodeling. Bone 2010: 46; 49-63. Copyright Elsevier 2010.*

It's not just complicated physiologic models that are difficult to explain, however. Even a relatively simple model, like the cell proliferation model shown in Figure 3, which has just a couple of feedback mechanisms, can cause a nonmodeler's eyes to bug out. Herein lies part of the problem with models. Most models require a certain degree of complexity to be useful. We are all familiar with Einstein's mass-energy equivalence equation, $E = mc^2$, and Newton's law of motion, $F = ma$, both of which are deceptively simple; however, there are few useful equations that can be described so succinctly. Figure 2 may well be impossible to communicate

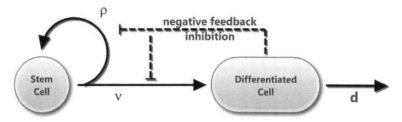

Figure 3. Model of stem cell differentiation as reported by Rodriguez-Brenes, Wodarz, and Komarova (2013).

to others in a simple manner. Figure 3 is a model reported by Rodriguez-Brenes, Wodarz, and Komarova (2013) for stem cell differentiation. Stem cells either divide at rate v with probability ρ into either two daughter cells or two differentiated cells, which themselves die at rate d. Both the rate of cell division v and the probability of self-renewal into daughter cells ρ are controlled by the number of differentiated cells. On its face, this model appears not to be that complicated but trying to explain how the factors interact to a layperson can stymie even the most experienced modelers. We, as modelers, have to find ways to present both simple and complicated models or equations to an audience in a way that is engaging, explanatory, and makes the audience enthusiastic towards our models such that they want to use them.

The comedian Bill Burr asked why is it that when really bad stuff happens in our lives we persevere, we tell ourselves "Okay. This is bad, but I'm going to get through this," yet, when we are stuck at a traffic light or in an endless line at the bank, we say to ourselves "Oh, God, kill me now. Please. Put me out of my misery." Being at a boring presentation should be added to that list of miseries. I don't know about you but I can't tell you how many presentations I've sat through that I thought the same thing, "Please, someone, put me out of my misery and don't make me sit through another minute of this." Sure there is some humor in this and we don't really want to die nor, I am sure, does the presenter want you to either, but boredom does have its consequences. Researchers have found that "those who report being bored are more likely [37% more] to die younger than those who are not bored" (Britton and Shipley, 2010). Now, granted, we could go into the whole debate about cause and effect and whether boredom is really the culprit, but that would be missing the point. which is, we don't want to bore our audiences. We want to keep them engaged, which can be hard because mathematical models are far from being the most dynamic topic. All the same, it is our job to present our results and not be boring while doing so.

This simple lesson took me a long time to learn. After years of frustration I realized that modeling was more than developing models and presenting them to an audience. There was a whole human side to presentations that I was completely ignoring. This psychological and personal component was as important, maybe even more important, than the models themselves and I wasn't considering either of these things during my presentations. I thought I could go in, give my presentation, and everyone would realize how incredible the model was. I was wrong. Very wrong. I needed to be more than a modeler. I needed to be a salesman. I needed to sell my models. It was then that I started to read and learn more about the art of selling. This has led me to read books on how to give effective presentations, social psychology, economics, and many other fields that were foreign to me when I started on this journey. Now, when I enter a room to give a presentation, I have a different mindset. I am not just a modeler. I am a salesman - I sell models.

That is what this book is about. It's about being more effective at presenting mathematical models, but not in the "here is how to make a graph" sense. It's more about the human side of presenting models and understanding how personal relationships, sales psychology, economics, business, and social psychology interact to make you a better model communicator (pun intended). This book is broken down as follows.

Chapter 2 deals with why models are difficult to sell. That answer may be obvious to some, but not to others. It's basically that most people don't understand models. They don't know how to evaluate them. They don't know how to interpret their results. They don't know when it is appropriate or inappropriate to use them. Because of this, people treat models as either heroes or villains. Let me give you a quick example. For 30 years the Black-Scholes equation, which governs the price of a stock option over time, was extremely useful allowing the sale of stock options as a commodity, making it a hero. Scholes was eventually awarded the Nobel Prize in Economics. Later, the model started to be abused and was used to trade derivatives, which are essentially contracts between two or more parties. They assume a value or "bet" on a value that is calculated or guessed at based on the value of the underlying assets which are frequently stocks, bonds, commodities, or currencies. Derivatives are useful because they can be used to protect high risk ventures, and the Black-Scholes equation, in particular, allowed derivatives to be traded just like commodities. In 2007, it was estimated that a quadrillion dollars (10-times the total worth of all manufactured products in the last century when adjusted for inflation) in derivatives were being traded.

As everyone is well aware, towards the end of the 2000s a financial crash shook the world-wide economy and pundits went scrambling looking for reasons why. Ian Stewart of *The Observer* claimed that the Black-Scholes equation was "the mathematical equation that caused the crash" (Embrechts, 2009). All modelers know that when predictions are made based on a model the validity of the model assumptions and the stability of the predictions needs to be assessed. As more and more risky derivatives began to be traded, no one really examined whether the model assumptions were still appropriate. "It worked in the past, it'll work in the future" was the mantra traders were using. Until it doesn't work, like in the Black-Scholes case, and everything starts to unravel. Chapter 2 presents other examples of this hero-villain dichotomy and sets the stage for the remainder of the book on how to be a model communicator.

Chapter 3 deals with the importance of establishing with your audience both trust (does the audience believe in you) and credibility (does the audience believe your message). When you give a presentation you are always being judged by your audience. They are always asking themselves

"Do I trust the speaker? Do I believe what they are saying?" While trust and credibility often go hand-in-hand, they don't necessarily have to. There are many examples of unscrupulous experts who have high credibility. Bernie Madoff was a highly regarded financier until it was discovered in 2008 that his asset management firm was a massive Ponzi scheme or "one big lie" as his son told investigators. James Grigson was a pathologist and a well-respected expert witness who testified in 167 capital murder trials, almost all of which resulted in death sentences. In 1995, he was expelled from the American Psychiatric Association for unethical conduct due to making psychiatric diagnoses without ever having met the defendant and for testifying in court that he could predict with 100% certainty whether an individual would commit future criminal acts. On the other hand, history is replete with examples of individuals who are trustworthy but rose to a level of incompetence that brought them down (*The Peter Principle*[1] in action). One example is Michael D. "Heck of a job, Brownie" Brown, who was Undersecretary of Emergency Preparedness and Response during the Bush Administration, and whose bungling of the New Orleans relief efforts in 2005 after Hurricane Katrina made national headlines.

As a speaker you want to achieve a high degree of trust and credibility with the audience. Would you buy a car from someone you trusted but whose product you didn't know well? Maybe. On the other hand, would you buy a car from someone who really knew the car but wasn't trustworthy? Probably not. The same holds true for scientific data. You wouldn't necessarily believe someone you didn't trust and you probably wouldn't use a model if the presenter didn't appear to be an expert in modeling. It's this simple – you must learn how to quickly form short-term trust and establish credibility and then build on that to establish long-term trust and credibility. Chapter 3 discusses ways to establish trust and credibility with an audience.

---

[1] Simply stated, *The Peter Principle* is a management theory that states that people rise in the hierarchy of an organization until they reach their level of incompetence.

Chapter 4 is about collaboration. Working with others to develop the model and leveraging that relationship to get greater model acceptance by larger groups, such as project teams. Modeling is largely a solitary activity and models that are developed by a single person are limited in the sense that few individuals have the same level of investment in the model as the modeler. This makes the model harder to sell. Models that are developed collaboratively have greater acceptance amongst teams because, not only were members of the collaborative team involved in building the model, they bring whatever trust, credibility, and influence they have to the larger project team or audience making it easier to sell. Collaboratively developed models also tend to be more evolved in the sense that a model developed by a single person is limited to the knowledge and skills of that one individual, but a model developed by an interdisciplinary team is based on a broader knowledge and skill set.

Chapter 5 is about preparing for your presentation, which includes creating the slide deck and rehearsing. A majority of scientists focus, almost exclusively, on the former and spend too little time on the latter. The presentation should be focused on what the audience wants or needs to see and not on what the modeler wants to show. It should be audience-centric, laser-focused, and should include a slide deck that follows the 5 C's: consistent, clear, concise, cultured, and content. Being well prepared is an old adage that applies to public speaking as well. A well prepared speaker knows their material, makes few gaffs during the presentation, and is cool and confident on the day of the presentation.

Chapters 6 and 7 are about the day you stand in front of an audience to give your presentation. For most people this is the scary part, with about 75% experiencing some form of anxiety or nervousness during a presentation. It doesn't have to be this way. Overcoming your fear of public speaking starts with the lessons learned in earlier chapters: gaining trust, establishing credibility, having an audience-centric, laser-focused slide deck, and being well rehearsed. It then moves onto presenting your material in a manner appropriate to the audience and concluding with a strong question and answer session.

How to present in front of a live audience will differ depending upon audience size. For example, you wouldn't give the same presentation to a large audience as you would a small audience because larger audiences are less intimate and more formal. Smaller audiences have a level of intimacy that allows give and take during the presentation between the speaker and audience as questions and concerns are raised. You wouldn't give the same type of presentation to a group with decision-making authority as you would to a single individual with that authority. Knowing how to tailor your presentation to the setting will increase your chances of a successful, informative presentation.

Chapter 7 explains how to answer questions, handle criticism, and resolve conflict during your presentation. After you finish your talk, or maybe even during, there may be lots of questions, some of which aren't really questions, but are, instead, criticisms of the model. This may lead to conflict between the modeler and team members. A confident speaker handles these questions with poise, addresses criticism, and resolves conflicts when the issues and concerns cannot be fully addressed.

Scientists today aren't adequately prepared for presenting scientific data. They give too few oral presentations while in school and are forced to learn how to present their models and data while on the job through trial and error. Some get better over time, some do not. Some learn the secrets of giving an effective and informative presentation that engages an audience. Others never really stop and think about the audience at all. They never stop to consider "what does the audience want to see?" Instead, their hubris gets in the way and they focus on the question "what can I show the audience?" That is not the same thing. The former is audience-centric, the latter is presenter-centric. Which do you think will be more successful?

Becoming a better presenter starts with awareness. Awareness of the audience, their level of technical expertise, their wants, their needs, and their feelings. Awareness of your strengths and limitations as a presenter. Awareness of your material. Awareness of what you want as the outcome of your presentation. Only from awareness can change be made. As you become more aware that there is more to modeling than modeling itself, you begin to realize that, to truly have impact in an organization you have to focus on more than just the model. The model is just a tool, not an end in and of itself. Too many people think that the model is the final product of an analysis. It is not. The model is just one part. It's how you present the model and its conclusions to others that is the real secret to success. You can be a very technically competent modeler but if no one understands you, are you really having an impact? Once you realize that communication is the real key to success, only then will you start on the path to becoming a model communicator.

The Game of Risk

We deal with probability everyday in our lives. What is the probability of rain? What are my chances of winning the lottery? What are my chances of having a car accident? Despite probability being so important in our lives, many people don't understand it, how to interpret it, or how it can impact their lives.

Challenge: As you proceed through the book, think about how you might explain to someone the concept of probability and then how you might explain to them the probability of some event happening based on a model you developed, like the chance of having a myocardial infarction after taking some new medication. What role might the model play in this explanation? How would you explain the model?

Extra Credit: Risk is the probability of an event and the consequences of that event. How might you explain to someone who knows nothing about probability the difference between probability and risk and then explain to them what are the risks associated with taking a new medication?

– Two –
They Just Don't Understand

Model usage surrounds us everyday of our lives. We wake up and check the weather. Is it going to rain today? How cold is it going to be? We get in our car and program the GPS. How long will it take to reach our destination and what is the shortest route? We get to work and check on our 401(k) retirement plan. How is our retirement account expected to perform in the next six months? Should we make any adjustments? Later that day we stop at our doctor's office for our physical. The doctor tells us that based on our cholesterol and LDL results, our risk for coronary heart disease is too high and given our weight she wants to start us on a higher than normal dose of a cholesterol lowering drug. When we go to the pharmacy to pick up our medicine, we grab some milk on the way out.

With each of these tasks, models are involved. Most of the time we don't even know that a model was used to solve a problem. Weather services use nonlinear partial differential equations to predict whether it will rain and what the high-low will be for the day. Our GPS uses a shortest-path optimization algorithm to find the shortest route and then uses our average speed and distance to calculate the time it will take to get to our destination. Economic models are used to predict how well our pension fund will do in the future. Algorithms used to assess the risk for heart attack or stroke are based on epidemiological models. The dosage of a drug prescribed to a patient is based on models relating dosage to efficacy, minimizing the risk to benefit ratio. Stores use point-of-sale inventory tracking and time series analysis to predict how much product should remain on hand and how often it should be reordered to ensure that products, like milk or prescriptions, do not run out and that little is thrown out due to spoilage. To most people these models are invisible in their everyday lives.

If models are all around us, why then are they so hard to sell? It's simple really – most people don't understand them. It took me a long time to recognize this. Most people, when presented with a model, don't know how to evaluate it or what questions should be asked. Does the model meet its objectives? Is the model being used appropriately? How was the model developed? What assumptions were made in developing the model? What are the limitations of the model? What was the range of data used to build the model and does the current prediction dataset result in interpolation or extrapolation of the model? How precise are the results? Few people know to ask these basic questions. They certainly don't care about "residuals" or "goodness of fit" plots. Because of this ignorance, most people are unable to challenge the model and its results. As a result, for most people, models are either angels or demons, heroes or villains, right or wrong. They either put too much trust in the model, and blindly believe the model's results, or are too distrustful and don't believe the model's results at all.

Now, I know you're thinking, *Isn't that a bit of an exaggeration? Angels and demons? That's just literary hyperbole.* Maybe. Let's look at a few examples before you decide. First, consider the Yucca Mountain Nuclear Waste Repository. The United States has a nuclear waste problem. Commercial nuclear power plants, nuclear weapon plants, nuclear submarines, and nuclear research facilities all produce radioactive waste through their use. In 2011, it was reported that there was 65,000 tons of nuclear waste in more than 100 temporary storage facilities throughout the

Figure 4. Yucca Mountain, Nevada, which has been called the "most studied real estate on the planet," was the proposed site for all nuclear waste disposal in the United States until the project was terminated in 2010 (The Majority Staff of the Senate Committee on Environment and Public Works, 3-1-2006). *Image reprinted from Wikipedia, Yucca Mountain.*

United States. In the 1950s the National Academy of Science (NAS) recommended that the best solution for radioactive waste removal, while at the same time protecting the public health and the environment, was deep underground burial of the material. This conclusion was reaffirmed in 2001 by another NAS panel. In the late 1970s the Department of Energy began studying potential sites, and in 1986 Yucca Mountain, which sits like a speed bump in the Armargosa Desert just north of Death Valley and approximately 100 miles northwest of Las Vegas, was chosen (Figure 4).

Yucca Mountain was picked as the number one choice in terms of hydrogeology, geochemistry, weather, rock characteristics, tectonics, cost, and societal impact. Between 1987 and 2002, the DOE spent close to another four billion dollars on scientific and technical studies of the mountain employing more than 2500 scientists over this period. A two mile tunnel was drilled to help with experiments in the rock itself creating the world's largest underground laboratory. Rock samples were collected, weather patterns and potential groundwater paths were studied, the adsorption of radionuclides on site minerals was characterized, the radionuclides were studied, and a myriad of other studies were also conducted.

In 2001, the U.S. Environmental Protection Agency (EPA) issued their guidelines for what they considered safe standards at Yucca Mountain: a dose limit of 15 mrem per year for the public outside the Yucca Mountain area. To put this into perspective, an average person receives about 1 mrem per day or 360 mrem per year in background sources. The standards were based on three components: individual exposure, human intrusion into the disposal area, and a groundwater component that was based on the EPA's Safe Drinking Water Guidelines which assumes water disposal standards are to apply for a period of 10,000 years after Yucca Mountain is sealed and closed.

Shortly after the guidelines were issued, the State of Nevada, the nuclear industry, and several public interest groups filed lawsuits in federal court challenging the guidelines. In 2004 the court ruled for the EPA on all counts except one thing, the 10,000 year limit. The judge ruled that the 10,000 year limit wasn't consistent with a statutory law requiring that the limit be consistent with NAS recommendation that guidelines be based on when peak exposure might be expected to occur, which could be as long as one million years. Hence, in 2009, the EPA amended the guideline with new limits of 15 mrem per year for the first 10,000 years and then 100 mrem per year from 10,000 to one million years after sealing and closing Yucca Mountain.

To determine whether the public would exceed these exposure limits, the Earth and Environmental Sciences Division of Los Alamos National Laboratory (LANL) began developing and validating a finite-element heat- and mass-transport (FEHM) model that solves the equations for heat and mass transport in 2- or 3-dimensions in either gas or liquid phase. This model, which is highly nonlinear and coupled, has been expanded, reviewed, modified, and validated based on experimental results for the last 30 years. It consists of 450 subroutines and 200,000 lines of computer code and accounts for many factors, including dissolving waste, radionuclide diffusion into solid matrices, sorption and desorption onto colloids, colloid transport, dissolving solids, solubility and speciation of different radionuclides, and precipitation from groundwater, just to name a few. With regards to Yucca Mountain, the model accounts for the different soil layers, mineral compositions, porosity, fracture densities, hydrogeological data, rock matrix and fracture permeability, and precipitation infiltration along the mountain's surface.

In a nutshell, LANL scientists have modeled the probability over time that rainwater will drip onto the canisters housing the radioactive waste and corrode them. As the canisters erode some of the radionuclides in the canisters will dissolve into the rainwater and be carried away into the soil and rock, eventually making its way to the aquifer, located 800 ft. below, and contaminating it. From there, the contaminated water might seep into a family's well and they might drink the water. Taking into account disaster scenarios like exploding volcanoes and the possibility of another ice age, scientists have estimated that the exposure to the leaked radionuclides in a hypothetical family won't rise above 15 mrem for hundreds of thousands of years.

For the advocates of using Yucca Mountain as a nuclear waste disposal site, the FEHM model was an angel allowing them to hide behind its arcane math, vast documentation, and colorful graphs like a shield. The model was never seriously challenged but a few did voice their concerns (Macfarlane and Ewing, 2006; Pilkey and Pilkey-Jarvis, 2007). In 2009, President Obama announced that Yucca Mountain was no longer an option and proposed cancelling the project, not because of any challenge to the model or its predictions, but for political reasons. The "not in my backyard" contingent led by Nevada Senator Harry Reid had won despite Republican opposition.

But why? Why was it that the model was never seriously challenged? Let's be honest, how many modelers would feel comfortable making a prediction a million years into the future? A million years is but a flash in the lifetime of the earth. A million years ago is when it was proposed that humans first used fire. Who knows what it will be like 10,000 years from now, let alone a million years. Why was the model never seriously challenged by Senator Reid and other opponents? Probably because he and his staff did not have the technical expertise to understand the model. After all, these were the guys that helped develop the atomic bomb. Who were they to challenge them? So they fell in line behind the scientists at LANL, never seriously questioning the uncertainties and assumptions of the model. They probably also realized that cancellation of the project would not be fought by technical experts arguing on the validity of a model, but by politics.

That was an example of a model as an angel. Now let's consider an example of a model as a demon. In the 1980s Wall Street had a problem. It wasn't enough to know the probability of a company going bankrupt. One had to know if a company went bankrupt whether it increased or decreased the probability of other companies going bankrupt as well. This is a correlation problem and "quants," as they were called on Wall Street, were stumped as to how to estimate these correlations. However David Li in 2000, who a couple of years later would be called the world's greatest actuary (which is ironic considering how this story ends), published a paper on how to estimate these joint probabilities using copulas (Figure 5), which estimate the joint probability distribution for two correlated random variables from their marginal distributions (Li, 2000). His equation allowed companies to correlate associations between multiple securities, like mortgages, bonds, banknotes, and derivatives, which had a profound impact on the financial industry. People were using words like *beautiful* to describe his model. By using Li's copula and repackaging high risk mortgages into triple-A rated investments, financial companies could, for the first time, manage their risk and at first, the Gaussian Copula was an angel as Wall Street firms made tons of money using it.

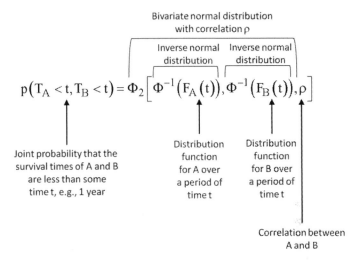

$$p(T_A < t, T_B < t) = \Phi_2\left[\Phi^{-1}(F_A(t)), \Phi^{-1}(F_B(t)), \rho\right]$$

Figure 5. David Li's Gaussian Copula (Li, 2000) – the formula credited for killing your 401(k) by Wired Magazine (Salmon, 2009).

As the real estate market collapsed, the mortgage industry collapsed and the world experienced a financial crisis that threatened to collapse entire economies. Trillions of dollars were lost and the entire global banking system seemed in jeopardy of imploding. Everyone asked, *how could this have happened?* The answer, many believed, was David Li and his Gaussian copula formula. Li's equation was made a scapegoat and it was widely reported in the press like Wired magazine (Salmon, 2009), the Financial Times (Jones, 4-24-2009), and the Wall Street Journal (Whitehouse, 9-12-2005) that Li's Copula caused this mess. Li's Copula became a demon of the first degree. Wired magazine reported that Li's equation "killed your 401(k)." People thus became aware that the reason they had lost so much money was because of a model. Li himself moved back to China in 2007, I suspect to escape the public lynching he was in for if he had stayed in the United States.

The problem with Li's equation was that the correlation between financial quantities (ρ in Figure 5) is inherently unstable and Li's equation made no accommodation for such uncertainty. Besides, the equation worked 99% of the time. However, for the 1% of the time when it didn't work, it failed spectacularly, and all gains that had been made earlier could be erased and further losses made. As Felix Salmon points out in his story in Wired:

> *"Bankers should have noted that very small changes in their underlying assumptions could result in very large changes in the correlation number. They also should have noticed that the results they were seeing were much less volatile than they should have been—which implied that the risk was being moved elsewhere. Where had the risk gone? They didn't know, or didn't ask. One reason was that the outputs came from "black box" computer models and were hard to subject to a commonsense smell test. Another was that the quants, who should have been more aware of the copula's weaknesses, weren't the ones making the big asset-allocation decisions. Their managers, who made the actual calls, lacked the math skills to understand what the models were doing or how they worked. They could, however, understand something as simple as a single correlation number. That was the problem."*

However much the press wanted to blame the model, the truth is that it wasn't Li's equation that caused the problem. Many of the managers who used the equation didn't understand it, people got greedy, and misapplied it to situations where it didn't apply. Li himself was very upfront about its limitations and said in 2005, in the Wall Street Journal, that "very few people understand the essence of the model." One mathematician has likened the public reaction to the Li equation to saying that this is like blaming the destruction from a nuclear bomb on Einstein's $E=mc^2$ equation (Stewart, 2-11-2012). I liken this analogy to the old slogan "Guns don't kill people, people do." Models don't kill your 401(k), people do. The story of blaming an equation is far more interesting than the other side of the story in which nebulous unnamed managers used an equation inappropriately, probably out of convenience, greed or ignorance.

Both Yucca Mountain and the Gaussian Copula story are both a little esoteric, and the fact that most people don't understand them should not be surprising. So let's now move on to something a little closer to home. Consider a model that most people use every day – weather models. Is it going to rain today? What about tomorrow? How hot will it be? To answer these questions, people may go to a variety of different sources like the newspaper, the local news, the TV, or the internet. They may even check multiple sources like The Weather Channel and the local news. Whatever the source, most people don't even think about it when the temperature is accurately predicted or it rains when they said it would rain. What they remember is when the predictions were wrong.

Weather forecasts are actually quite special because most people realize that forecasts are based on a model. Some people even know that different models are used by different sources of weather information. The local newspaper may use the National Weather Service while the local radio may use AccuWeather, which utilize two different models. So one source can say one thing, while another can say something different. Since you don't necessarily know whom to believe, this leads to a credibility issue amongst all the sources. Then there is the issue of accuracy, which goes hand in hand with credibility. None of the models have the same accuracy (Table 1).

ForecastAdvisor, a company that compiles weather accuracy statistics, reported that in downtown Chicago in 2012, the National Weather Service was accurate in predicting rain 74% of the time. Of course, just assuming it will rain tomorrow given that it is raining today (this is called the persistence method) was accurate 55% of the time. Hence, just assuming it will rain tomorrow given that it is raining today, you will be right about half the time. The use of the model increases the accuracy of rain prediction from about 50% to right around 75%. Ultimately, you have a situation where you don't know who to believe because different models perform better under different conditions and whatever source you finally do choose to believe is not completely reliable. This is why most of the time people choose whatever source is most convenient for their weather information and then take the attitude "expect the unexpected."

Provider (model)	High Temperature	Low Temperature	Rain or Snow
Intellicast	65%	70%	75%
The Weather Channel	65%	71%	75%
National Weather Service	62%	63%	74%
NWS Digital Forecast	63%	67%	70%
AccuWeather	57%	59%	76%
Persistence	31%	32%	55%

Table 1. Accuracy of weather predictions in Chicago from April 2012 to April 2013. *Source: www.forecastadvisor.com, accessed April 2013. Accuracy of high and low temperature based on observed temperature being within ±3°F of prediction.*

What is perhaps not all that surprising about weather predictions is that despite their constant presence in our lives, not everyone knows how to interpret them. In a recent story reported by National Public Radio (NPR) on understanding probability (7-22-2014), using a survey developed by the National Center for Atmospheric Research, they queried listeners about their ability to understand simple weather predictions. Given the statement that tomorrow's forecast calls for a "20% chance of rain[2]," only slightly more than half got the answer correct ("It will rain on 20% of the days like tomorrow"). Similarly when asked what does it mean when it is stated that "rain is likely tomorrow," again, only slightly more than half got the question right ("It will rain likely at any one point in the forecast area"). What is scary about these results is that the average listener of NPR has an above-average education with more than half having a college degree.

Now that a few examples of models being angels and demons have been presented, let's go back to the original question: why is it that models are difficult to sell to people? I believe that many people have an inherent distrust in them. Some may argue that its not the models that are distrusted,

---

[2] How many people realize that rain is defined by the National Weather Service as "1/100 an inch of precipitation?" This is 6-times the thickness of a penny.

Figure 6. Where there is trust, great things can happen. Above: Anwar Sadat (left, President of Egypt), Jimmy Carter (middle, President of the United States), and Manachem Begin (right, Prime Minister of Israel) in 1979 at the White House after signing of the Israel-Egypt Peace Accord, which has led to over 30 years of peace between the two countries. *Image reprinted with permission from the Jimmy Carter Library and Museum.*

experiential and situational component to credibility. Credible people have the experience and the expertise to back up what they are saying. While being an expert in an area is one way to get credibility with an audience, paradoxically, one of the most tangible ways to gain credibility with an audience is to admit "I don't know" when you don't know something. Most audiences can sense when someone is acting like they know something when they don't. To admit that you don't know something is a sign of honesty to an audience they might not be used to receiving and may find it a sign of trustworthiness or credibility. Of course, if you are asked something you don't know, you must find out what the answer is afterwards and then follow up with the questioner with the answer.

Credibility and trust frequently go together but do not necessarily go hand in hand. Someone can be credible but we may not trust them, or we may trust them but think they are not credible. Tiger Woods and George Tenet are two examples of the potential dichotomy between trust and credibility.

Tiger Woods has great credibility in golf after winning many Master's tournaments, but he might not be considered that trustworthy because of the many times he cheated on his wife. Conversely, George Tenet was director of the Central Intelligence Agency (CIA) when George Bush was president. It was his agency that concluded that Iraq had weapons of mass destruction, which eventually led to the United States invading Iraq and toppling Saddam Hussein. George Tenet is an example of a trustworthy man who had little credibility after it was realized that the CIA assessment was wrong. Thereafter, all CIA conclusions he reported were treated as suspect in the eyes of the public. What about when trust and credibility *do* go hand in hand? Steve Jobs, cofounder, chairman, and CEO of Apple, Inc., was one such example. When Steve Jobs took over at Apple, the company was nearly bankrupt. Through his credibility and the trust his staff and Wall Street gave him, they turned the company around into one of the biggest success stories of the century. When trust and credibility go hand in hand the results can be very powerful.

It should be recognized, however, that trust is a behavior that applies across all situations – you either trust someone or you don't – but credibility tends to be situational. A person may be credible in one area but not credible in another. A weatherman may have more credibility at predicting what the weather will be, but is only as credible as the next guy at predicting the next president. Sometimes, however, a person's trustworthiness may spill over into their credibility. A person may be so trustworthy that it increases their credibility. When someone gives a presentation to a group, for the presenter's message to be believed, the presenter must be someone who has both the trust of the group and is a credible source. Would you buy something from someone you distrusted? Probably not. Would you listen to someone who wasn't credible? Probably not. When you distrust someone, you scrutinize every aspect of their presentation looking for mistakes and confirmation that they are wrong.

Some people think that trust can be earned. Indeed, some micromanagers believe that by repeatedly showing over time they are trustworthy, they have earned the trust of others. In reality, trust is given. We give our trust to others and people choose to give their trust to us. Implied in this is that someone can withdraw their trust. Some people give their trust more freely than others and some countries are just more trusting than others (Zak, 2008). In a response to the question, "Do you think people can be trusted?" more than half the respondents in Norway, Denmark, and China responded in the affirmative. The United States was about 35%, Japan about 40%, and Great Britain about 28%. Bringing up the rear was Brazil at about 3%.

When new teams form and the presenter is meeting a team for the first time, uncertainty and doubt prevail about the team members or the new team member (Harrison-McKnight and Chervany, 2006). In the absence of hard evidence for a person's credibility and trustworthiness, we tend to rely on first impressions. First impressions matter a great deal because, not only are they formed in a matter of seconds, they tend to last. This is an evolutionary mechanism we all have. We need to size someone up quickly and determine whether they are a friend or a foe. Can they be trusted? A negative first impression is difficult to overcome because once someone is seen negatively, everything they do is viewed through that lens. If you view someone negatively, if that someone makes a mistake, that's just confirmation to you that they are incompetent. This is called 'attribution bias' and is a fundamental error in the way people think. It can't be avoided unless you consciously examine every decision you make. Conversely, we don't like to change our positive opinion of someone because that would indicate that maybe we misjudged them or the situation and we don't like to think that we are the kind of person who might misjudge others. That might call into question all our other decisions.

So how do you make a good first impression? It's based on how you look and how you act. Whether you smile and are open to others, what you say and how you respond to criticism and questions. The most important thing you can do is be confident but not to the point of being arrogant. Whether someone is confident is easy to tell. They are relaxed. They don't slouch. They smile. They make eye contact. Their voice projects. They are passionate and enthusiastic when they speak. They don't look afraid and they don't fidget. Public speaking is stressful, even for the best of us, and a person that projects being calm and in control generates an aura of confidence. In order to project confidence, it helps to think positively. Tell yourself that you know this material better than anyone in the room. Visualize yourself as being a success. It can't be stressed enough that you also need to be prepared. A brilliant speaker who is not prepared cannot save the presentation. The stereotype of the guy that wings a great oratory at the end of a movie to great success with no preparation is a pure fiction of Hollywood.

You need to look confident. The old saying about dressing for success may be a cliché, but it is an accurate cliché. You should dress at least as well as the people in the room to whom you are presenting. It's better, though, if you are the best dressed person in the room but not to the point of overdoing it. If an office dresses business casual, you should dress business casual. If an office dresses in business suits, you should dress in a business suit. Dressing better also makes you feel better and makes you feel more confident. It's important to know your audience, what they wear, and how well they relate to what you are wearing. Think of the colors you wear. Some colors are warm like yellows, brown, and warm reds. Cool colors are blues, green, pink, and purple. Warm colors like red and yellow evoke feelings of warmth and comfort. Cool colors like blue and green are thought of as calming, but can also be thought of as indifference. You should wear a color that makes you feel good, one that gives you confidence, but is appropriate for the audience. Companies that are cutting edge may be more forgiving with bold colors but established companies may require more subdued, traditional colors. Whatever you wear make sure it's not too busy and does not detract from your presentation.

It has been reported that most of our communication is by nonverbal means and can play an important role in judging whether someone is credible or not, whether they are truthful or not (Mehrabian and Ferris, 1967). How we stand or sit is an important signal to others (Driver, 2010). If you stand in a neutral and balanced position with the solar plexus open, you are deemed more open and approachable than if you stand off-center with your arms closed or folded. Good communicators relax their arms and frequently use them for added expression, showing their palms. If you are sitting you should lean forward resting your arms on the table, parallel, with your solar plexus open. Again, these cues work to increase credibility, trustworthiness, and approachability.

One of the most important nonverbal cues is eye contact. We feel more confident that when someone looks us in the eye, they are not lying to us. Excessive blinking, looking right or left, looking at the floor or ceiling are unconscious signals that someone is not being honest. This doesn't mean stare at someone like a lizard – maintain sincere eye contact with people. Also keep in mind that in some cultures, like the Japanese, it is not proper to look a superior in the eye, so there are cultural contexts to these cues. A relaxed face and posture are signs of confidence and honesty. Don't scratch your face. Remember Pinocchio – every time he told a lie his nose grew. Excessive touching of the face is a sign to people of dishonesty or insecurity. What is interesting about these cues is that they are learned at a very early age, as early as two years (Birch et al., 2010).

Now that we know some of the things we should be doing to gain initial trust, are there things we should avoid doing, things that cause us to lose credibility and trustworthiness? While some may think those people who do not look them in the eye or those people who fidget too much are not trustworthy, in truth, some signals we use to assess trustworthiness are far more subtle. David DeSteno and colleagues at Northeastern University (2012) showed that when people meet for the first time, those people who crossed their arms in a block fashion, leaned away from the other person, touched their bodies like on their shirt or arms, or rubbed their hands together while they talked were less likely to be considered trustworthy. By themselves, these gestures didn't signal any warnings but in combination they triggered some primitive emotion that was picked up on by the other person and the more frequently these gestures occurred the more untrustworthy the person appeared.

What can we learn from this study? Clearly, we should not use the cues that are unconscious warning signs during our initial social interactions with people. When you are giving your presentation, be open, don't cross your arms, don't rub your hands, and refrain from touching your face or elsewhere on your body. Will this guarantee trust? No, but it will go towards you not being deemed untrustworthy.

When we come into a new situation we must quickly establish trust with the other team members and this is done through rapidly establishing credibility within the team. However, the cues we use to assign credibility and trust when we first meet someone are not the same cues we use to determine whether someone is credible or trustworthy in the long run. Long-term trust is built over time by repeatedly showing you can be trusted.

When someone on a team is already recognized as trustworthy and credible, it makes it easier for the audience to receive the message. Even though trust is given, there are behaviors that can be used to facilitate long-term trust formation. During a presentation you are part salesman, part expert witness. You are trying to sell the audience your models while at the same time having the credibility of an expert witness. To facilitate trust as a salesman, Georges and Guenzi (2012) proposed five necessary behaviors:

- **Customer orientation**: the higher the customer orientation the higher the level of satisfaction. In modeling, customer orientation is meeting the needs of the project. Did you answer the question, solve the problem, or did you go off on some tangent in which the team was not interested? Is your presentation geared towards your audience, or is your presentation perhaps overly complex?

- **Selling orientation**: When you try too hard to sell a customer something, this produces a negative impact on trust. Don't push too hard in selling a model.

- **Expertise**: Expertise is your knowledge, your ability to answer questions, and perceived credibility. Greater expertise is associated with greater trust.

- **Likeability**: Likeability is your ability to connect to people on a positive emotional level. Mutual liking is a key to customer trust but is not sufficient to develop a good working relationship.

- **Dependability**: Dependability is your ability to deliver quality results in a timely manner.

Think of a witness in a jury trial and you are a member of the jury. Is the witness credible? Do you believe their testimony? In a sense, when you are new to a team and you are asked to make a presentation, you are like a witness in a trial. What are the factors you use to establish whether you think they are credible or not? Viewed in this light, you can use the general criteria used to evaluate whether a witness is credible or not. They are:

- **Trustworthiness**: Are they trustworthy? Do they appear honest? Are they worthy of your belief? These questions may be difficult to answer and there is a high degree of subjectivity, particularly with regards to nonverbal cues, in answering these questions.

- **Expertise**: You evaluate their background. Are they an expert? Do they have the skills and experience to do the work? Scientists tend to first look at degrees and titles. Do they have a PhD? A master's degree? What is their job title? Are they a full professor or an associate professor? They then look at past experience. Have they published in this area? They look to see if the presenter has the skills of an expert.

- **Credibility**: Do they act credible or believable? Are they consistent in their presentation? Are they confident? Does their work appear sound? Is their presentation clear and concise? Do they stand their ground on examination when they are questioned about their presentation and do they answer questions in a concise, clear manner with authority? If any of these questions are not answered in the affirmative, the presenter's credibility may be called into question.

- **Objectivity**: Do they appear unbiased about their work? There is an old saying "don't fall in love with your models." Modelers that are clearly in love with their model appear too biased and have less credibility than someone who appears objective about their work. Pointing out limitations of a model goes a long way towards establishing credibility with the audience, but may backfire because it detracts from the believability of the model.

- **Charisma**: This is very similar in concept to likeability. Are they dynamic when they present? Is there a certain degree of forcefulness and certainty in how they present their results? Charismatic people tend to be more liked than noncharismatic people and, by association, charismatic people are more believable. We like them so we want to believe them.

It is clear from George and Guenzi's five behaviors and the behaviors of an expert witness that there are some commonalities and over-arching themes. Stephen M.R. Covey in his classic book *The Speed of Trust* (2006) nicely generalizes these themes into four criteria (Figure 7) that are built around character and competence:

- **Integrity** (a character trait): Covey defined integrity as basically being honest and trustworthy. Without integrity there is no foundation for trust. Covey states that integrity requires three attributes: you have to be humble, you have to do what is right, and you have to have the courage to do what is right.

- **Intent** (a character trait): Intent is related to what are your motives and agenda? Trust increases if your motives are straight-forward and based on mutual goals or are in the best interest of others.

- **Capability** (a competence trait): Competence means you can do the job. To be capable you need to have the talent, proper attitude, knowledge, and style. Higher difficulty tasks require greater competence.

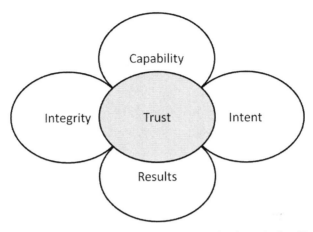

Figure 7. Stephen M.R. Covey in his New York Times bestselling book *The Speed of Trust* (2006) generalizes trust into these four themes

- **Results** (a competence trait): This is pretty self-explanatory. Do you produce results? If you do things on time, your credibility increases. Failure to do so decreases your credibility.

Notice that credibility is a combination of the subjective and objective. You have to *act* the part before you can *be* the part. Although sending the right signals is not a guarantee of acceptance, sending the wrong signals is a quick way to failure.

One thing that has been left out from Covey's criteria is likeability, the ability to create positive attitudes in others. Do you need to be liked to be trusted? The answer appears to be no. Being likeable means you are able to connect with people in a positive emotional manner. The Boston Globe in their obituary of Steve Jobs, the chairman of Apple, said Jobs "spread his unhappiness like a virus, abusing his friends, neglecting his family, [and] insulting and reviling his colleagues." The man was notorious for his reputation as a mean person and was quite unlikeable, yet people trusted him. Was Jobs the exception? No, others come readily to mind like Larry Ellison of Oracle or Simon Cowell from American Idol. So while it is not necessary to be likeable to be trusted, I would argue that it helps.

Tim Sanders (2006) wrote a book called *The Likeability Factor*. He said that "when the viewer likes your ad or brand, they assume you make a high quality product." The same can be said for work quality, in general. If a person likes you they assume you do a good job and can perform. If you are not likeable, it's hard for me to tell you to be more likeable. You either are or you aren't. Even so, you can try to work at increasing your likeability. Sanders says that the keys to increasing your likeability are friendliness (your openness to others), relevance (your ability to connect with other's wants, interests, and needs), empathy (your ability to recognize and connect the feelings of other people), and realness (your authenticity and integrity) in that order. In other words, you have to be friendly before you can be relevant, etc. A simpler key is to have a positive attitude and try to connect with others on an emotional level.

In today's work environment, it is not uncommon to have teams with members, located at different physical sites, interacting by the internet, telephone, or videoconference. Building trust with these virtual teams is harder because the visual cues normally used to establish trust with teams that are physically collocated are absent, or limited, because of the quality of the video/internet feed. Often times these virtual teams never meet in person. Some have argued that trust cannot be built unless there is face to face interaction. I disagree. I think trust can be built in virtual teams, just not by the same means as when face to face. Members need to form swift trust and then look for ways to build interpersonal trust. Social communication and communication that conveys enthusiasm are factors that rapidly build trust in virtual teams (Coppola et al., 2004). Often at the start of virtual meetings, there is a period where members are chatting, sometimes about the day's events, sometimes about events in their own lives. Use this time to build on those interpersonal relationships. We tend to trust people who are similar to us, so look for opportunities to build on similarities. If someone is discussing a concert they went to and you saw the show, even if it was years ago, bring that up. Tell them you saw the show and what you thought about it. Show interest in what others are talking about. Look for ways to build on empathy, but be careful not bring the focus of the conversation towards you. Be more interested in what people say than in being interesting yourself. Conversations don't have to be a tennis match. If someone is talking about a difficult experience they had, don't change the topic to a difficult experience you had. Empathize with them. Sometimes just acknowledging their difficulty and their experience is enough to help build trust. If you don't get the opportunity during meetings to form these interpersonal dynamics, phone calls outside of team meetings should be considered or use email if you are communicating with someone from another country where there may be verbal language difficulties.

Because your face is often not seen in meetings with virtual teams, how you speak is also important. Speak clearly, don't mumble, be confident, and smile at times. Even though we may not see your face people can still recognize when someone is smiling. Some recommend mirroring how team leaders speak on the phone as a way to build trust. I can't recommend this because it is difficult to do correctly and if you can't do it right, it will destroy your trust on the team because others may think you are making fun of them.

It has been said that communication builds trust, and this is true to a degree. In virtual teams, the importance of communication, particularly clarity and frequency of communication, cannot be overstated. Misunderstandings are a common way to kill trust on virtual teams, so do everything to avoid them. Follow-up on emails, phone calls, whatever is needed to ensure that you and others understand your role and tasks.

In addition to interpersonal relationships, team-related task-oriented activities within virtual teams also builds trust because virtual teams tend to be more goal-focused than physical teams. Peter Andrews of IBM Consulting (Andrews, 2004) says that for virtual teams, members must answer yes to three questions about each other for trust to form:

1. Can you help me?

2. Can I count on you?

3. Will you do the job the right way?

These questions are the pragmatic approach to trust – task oriented with no accounting of the human side of teams. The practical way to get affirmation on these questions is to use many of the same building blocks noted earlier to gain trust: topic-matter credibility, trustworthiness, acting in the team's best interests, adhering to deadlines, be engaged at team meetings, etc.

Many of the same factors used to establish trust face to face are used with virtual teams, it's just more difficult to establish interpersonal connections. As society becomes more virtual, we can expect to work more and more on virtual teams. Just look at kids today, they communicate mostly by text messages; phone calls are passé. These are the workers of tomorrow. Further, companies are encouraging more employees to work from home as a way to reduce costs. Virtual teams are thus increasingly common and as such, we need to be aware of the inherent limitations and difficulties in establishing trust in this setting and what can be done about it.

I am now going to give you the take home message for this chapter. It's the title of the chapter – trust and credibility are the foundation for all else. If you can get people to trust you and they believe you, you are half way to selling your model. This is not as simple as it sounds. Its cliché, I know, but trust isn't just handed out. It takes time to establish and is easily lost. Once you get it, people will follow you. That doesn't mean they will buy what you are selling, but consider the flip-side, without trust people won't buy what you are selling. Would you?

– Four –
Collaboration: or there's No "I" in Model

When I first started doing modeling in the pharmaceutical industry in the early 1990's, the modeler was an ancillary part of the project team, one of an extended team that provided scientific advice to the core decision-making body. If there were questions I thought could be answered by modeling, the project team basically gave me a pat on the head and said 'Okay, Pete, go ahead and build your model. Come back when you have one'. So off I went, alone in my office, to work on the model. I would come back and present the results to the team. Often they had questions. Some thought the model was too simplistic. Some thought the model was too complicated or had too many unverified assumptions. Some just didn't understand it. "Why are we doing this modeling thing?" some said. Sometimes they used my model in the decision-making process, sometimes they didn't. In either case, it was a frustrating process for me, personally, because I felt no support for what I was doing and felt that many on the project team were just humoring me. "What did it hurt if Pete went off and made a model? Run along now, Pete." Thankfully, things are better today. Modeling and simulation has become a largely accepted tool to aid in decision-making and is integral to the process in some companies and businesses. In many instances, though, modeling today is still a process that is done by some lone individual toiling away at a computer in seclusion. At the end of the process the modeler presents the results to the decision-making group, the project team in my instance, and their results are either accepted or rejected. By that I mean the results based on the models are either used in the decision-making process or are discounted and not used.

Everyone wants their opinion to be heard, even if the final decision is not what they wanted. This is called fair justice. Everyone also wants their work to be valued and considered important. They want to feel they contributed. Modeling is not easy. You go to all this effort and trouble and, if at the end of it all, your model is not used, it will make you feel unappreciated and maybe even a bit angry. Fair justice has not been served. Thankfully, there are things you can do to prevent your modeling results from being discounted; or at least you can tip the scales in your favor.

One way to have your opinion heard is to make your results essential to the decision-making process. If the model is the only way to answer a question that makes the model's results absolutely necessary and it is likely the model will be accepted more often than not. However, there are ways to answer a question besides modeling, like intuition. Intuition may not be the best (or most scientific) way to come to a decision, but there are many leaders who listen to all the data and recommendations from their advisors, throw it all away, and then base their decision on their gut instinct. If this is the situation you work in, you need to learn how to "Tame Your Hippo", which is discussed later in the book.

However, many times decisions are made by teams, and teams can be influenced. I have found the best way to get team support for a model is by exerting influence throughout the entire model development process, starting before you even think about what model to build all the way until the model is presented to the team. By starting at the very beginning and by using collaboration, the process by which individuals work together to reach a common goal, you can increase the odds your model will be used in the decision-making process.

Collaboration can have a huge impact and that impact is increasingly seen in science today. Think of, perhaps, the greatest scientific collaboration, for good or bad, in the 20th century – the Manhattan Project. Organized in 1942, its goal was to develop the atomic bomb. Hundreds of scientists and technicians were brought together across different sites with a single goal, to develop the bomb before the Germans did, which they achieved. No scientist or even a small group of scientists could have reached this goal by themselves. It needed the collective cooperation of all those involved to achieve success.

Unfortunately collaboration during the model development process does not always occur. By its nature, modeling is usually a solo endeavor. The modeler grinds away at the computer, alone, analyzing data, trying to find the best model to explain some data and then maybe using that model to predict something of interest. It's a difficult process to open up this solo activity to others in a meaningful way. Being a solo activity is not the only reason why collaboration does not occur. There are also other more general reasons:

- Collaboration takes effort and is more work. Who wants more work?

- What becomes of roles and responsibilities? Who takes claim for success? Who takes the blame for failure?

- People don't like going outside their comfort zone so there is a silo mentality in their approach to their job.

While there are many reasons not to collaborate, there are just as many reasons to collaborate and the benefits of collaboration far outweigh the added work and uncertainty. Most science today is too complex for any one person to know the entire subject matter of a discipline. Science is done at the team level. The individual scientist, like Alexander Graham

Bell, is a thing of the past. Big science, like the Manhattan Project or even small science at the level of a university professor, almost always requires collaboration. Research grants from granting bodies have a greater chance of success if the grant is collaborative rather than for an individual.

Collaborating on a model has one big advantage - ownership. People feel a sense that the model is theirs when they have a chance to participate in bringing that model to life. When they have participated in the model development process and feel that all their concerns have been addressed, they are more likely to accept the results and buy the model. There is little chance they will outright reject the results if they actively worked to develop the model. Also, if the results don't agree with their preconceived notions of what the model or the results should look like, they will go back and re-examine the assumptions that went into building the model and work to tweak it. They won't just ignore the results or discount them. Collaborating on a model also allows for synergistic model development where the additional team members provide their input into the structure and interpretation of the model. This synergy is particularly notable when members of the team are of diverse scientific disciplines, e.g., a modeler, pharmacologist, and physician. Thus, collaboration is a huge step towards model acceptance.

The importance of collaboration in science has given rise to a whole new field of study called Team Science[3], which is at the interface of psychology, management, and science, and is devoted to understanding how teams communicate, organize, and conduct collaborative, large-scale team based science. Why is this important? Because as scientists become more and more specialized it becomes more and more difficult for them to talk to scientists outside their field. All the jargon, the different methods, and the different research questions makes it hard for scientists to understand the problems in different areas and to discuss ways to solve

---

[3] The website http://www.scienceofteamscience.org/ is a useful resource on this new and exciting field.

Figure 8. Team science is the norm for modern research. Collaboration can create solutions that wouldn't have existed otherwise. *Image courtesy of Kate McCurrach (http://scientific-culture.blogspot.com/).*

those problems. Team science researchers focus on improving the collaborative process between scientists.

Collaboration in Model Development

The first step in a model-development collaboration is forming the team. Who are the members that will be involved in the collaborative effort? If all the members of the collaborative team are of the same scientific discipline this is referred to as a disciplinary team, but if the members are from different scientific disciplines this is referred to as a multidisciplinary team. A disciplinary team might be a group of modelers all working on the same model, whereas a multidisciplinary group might consist of biologists, modelers, chemists, and statisticians working on the model. The appropriate team depends on the problem at hand. There are advantages and disadvantages to whichever is chosen. With a disciplinary team, all members have the same fundamental assumptions and values. There is little need to worry about jargon as everyone understands the same meanings. However, a disciplinary team may be limited by the types of models known in the discipline. For example, groups of pharmacokinetic modelers tend to focus on compartmental models, since that is their training, but they may be unaware of the types of models being developed by systems biologists. Multidisciplinary teams, on the other hand, have a greater breadth of knowledge, not necessarily modeling knowledge, and tend to be more innovative than disciplinary teams. However they may be hampered by conceptual differences between disciplines and difficulties in communication since they all speak different disciplinary languages, which, as a consequence, may cause them to be slower than disciplinary teams (Eigenbrode et al., 2007).

True collaboration should be based on inclusion of the relevant stakeholders who impact the decision-making process. Deciding just who are those relevant stakeholders can be challenging. Straus (2002) recommends including those who can block any decision, those who have the authority to make a decision, those affected by the decision, and those with relevant information or expertise. While this recommendation may be useful for large-scale policy decisions, including all these individuals may create a group too large and unwieldy to be effective with regards to model development. Therefore, I recommend you invite those with relevant information and expertise and a few people with broad, overarching decision-making authority from the team or a few individuals with influence on the team. If you include a few decision makers and they agree with the model, often the other team members follow suit with regards to decision-making. Alternatively, if there is a team member who has influence with the team or is quite vocal in their criticism of models you may consider including them on the team as a pre-emptive strike against their complaints. If the difficult person doesn't agree with the model, they will be less likely to complain about it if they were on the team that built the model.

While on the surface it may appear that even having a limited size team is too unmanageable, as Straus points out, within any team there are members who are more involved with the process than others. Straus proposes that

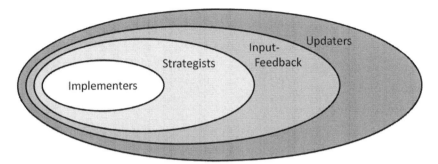

Figure 9. Schematic of Straus' (2002) Rings of Involvement.

team members sit in different "rings of involvement", and that the further a member gets out from the core of the team the less direct involvement they have on a daily basis. This allows more members to participate on the team without the team becoming too large.

Under Straus' model (Figure 9), the innermost ring contains the Implementers and may consist of just a modeler and computer programmer. Implementers do the day-to-day modeling activities and their goal is to carry-out the work recommended by the second ring of involvement, the Strategy ring. This latter group will include members of the Implementation ring, subject-matter experts, and may include important decision-makers from the larger project team. The Strategy ring helps develop the model development strategy (what data will be used, what models will be examined, etc.) while the implementers execute that strategy.

The Strategy ring is encircled by the Input-Feedback ring, which includes those individuals who want to provide input into the model (like what the model's structure should be or how well the model should perform, but may not know how) and those individuals who provide feedback on the model after the model is completed and evaluated. This latter group may include model experts. For example, if the model is a statistical model and this person is an expert in that particular type of statistical model, they may provide feedback on implementation of the model in a particular software system. Or, if the model is a mechanistic model and they are subject-domain experts, they may provide feedback on how well the model captures the system. The feedback group can be used as a sounding board. The last ring is the Update ring, those individuals who don't want to become involved in day-to-day development of the model but want to remain apprised of decisions and results of the collaborative team.

How much individuals are involved in the collaborative team depends on many factors, such as how interested they are in the project or the time commitment of the project. Individuals do not remain static in a ring but are able to go up and down from one ring to another. At one point in time a person may not have the time to be part of the strategy ring but may want to still remain informed of the group's decisions, but at a later point in time may move into the strategy ring to help guide model development.

Despite efforts to try and make a collaboration inclusive, it's rarely possible to have everyone on the decision-making team be part of the collaborative team. There will always be excluded individuals who, when presented with the model, may feel left out from model development and may reject the model out of spite or who may be completely blindsided by the results and reject the model because they don't understand it. For these individuals, it may be better to include them in the process than to exclude them, even if it's just at the level of the update ring, or you may want to influence them before you present the model to the team. If you have a personal relationship with an excluded team member, you can start by having casual conversations with them. "Let me tell you about the model we just built. I think it will really help the project team come to a better decision." Then as the conversation develops, they get a better understanding of the model, what it does, and what it means. If you don't have a personal relationship with them, you may still find it useful to set up a pre-meeting with them to discuss the model. This gives them an opportunity to ask questions and understand the methods and results without the pressure of being in a team setting. People are often very different when alone compared to being in a group, particularly if they are

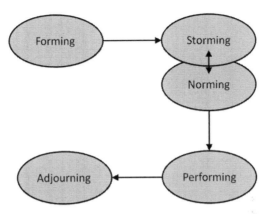

Figure 10. A modification of Bruce Tuckman's model of the life-cycle of a team that accounts for cycling back through phases.

a leader in a group. By being proactive you may turn them from an opponent into a proponent.

A large part of a collaboration is the search for solutions. To any particular problem there are often many solutions. Simply putting people together into a team – even the most talented people – and defining an objective is not enough to ensure that the objective is achieved. Teams go through stages starting from their formation, and each stage has a different degree of effectiveness. One such model of a team's life-cycle was proposed more than 40 years ago by Bruce Tuckman (1965) who coined the phrase "forming, storming, norming, performing" to describe the path teams follow on their road to reach high performance (Figure 10). A fifth stage, "adjourning," was added later.

At the Forming stage, which is usually a brief period, team members are introduced and are excited and anxious to be in the group. They are often sure they will find a solution to the problem they have been asked to solve. The next two stages, the Storming and Norming stage, have a considerable degree of overlap. The Storming stage can be characterized by conflict as team members compete for position within the group and different ideas and solutions compete against each other for consideration. A useful question to address in the Storming stage is "What are the personal ground rules for teamwork and collaboration on the team?" The level of commitment of team members to the team should be addressed. Everyone should agree to be honest with each other and speak up when they have an opinion. Everyone should agree to work with respect and to contribute to the project. You may want to discuss how conflict, tension, and debate will be resolved. Getting such agreements early should help to resolve team conflict.

In the Norming stage team members feel a sense of unity and cohesion. Expectations and roles are defined. Strategies to achieve team goals are agreed upon. Members start to accept responsibility to the team and mutual trust and understanding among team members is formed. Newly formed teams, with members that don't know each other, should take some time to discuss not only the project, but also introduce themselves in order to help build trust and relationships among team members. Conflict within the team should be accepted as a good thing at this stage and not taken personally.

Taking the time to build team relationships is helpful so that when things get difficult, the team has positive emotional energy to fall back on. You don't want a situation where failure of a team to agree on some point leads to anger and resentment in some members. A good way to build trust in a team is to set some easily achievable goals early on because reaching these goals will provide confidence for more difficult, long-term goals.

Unfortunately, some teams never leave these two stages as they fail to develop that sense of trust, unity, and organization. In order to help teams move into the Performing stage, here are some questions that should be answered:

- What are the objectives of the collaboration? The first question that should be answered is to define and agree upon the scope of the project. What will be accomplished by the collaboration and what does the team hope to achieve? Both short-term and long-term goals should be identified. Teams that don't identify and agree upon the project mission, and the tasks necessary to complete the mission, are at risk to be one of those kinds of teams that meets and never achieves anything. Further, without direct goals, enthusiasm will be limited and participation will be sporadic at best.

Often goal definition is overlooked when new collaborations are formed because it is assumed by the members that everyone knows what the goals and objectives are. Sometimes this may be true, more often than not everyone has a different view of what they are. The agreed upon goal(s) should be defined as quantitatively as possible so as to avoid ambiguity. For example, a model-based goal could be "to build a model in adults of the relationship between Drug X plasma concentrations and probability of seizures and to predict the probability of seizures in neonates when 100 mg Drug Y is coadministered with 30 mg Drug X."

- What are the steps necessary to achieve the goal and what are the timelines? What are the major and minor milestones? If you start to deviate from timelines who is responsible for getting the team back on track? A chart laying out timelines for each task may be useful to ensure timely delivery of results. An example timeline may be as simple as Data Collection (two weeks) → Data clean-up (two week) → Model development (two weeks) → Model validation (one week) → Report writing (two weeks).

- What modeling approach or approaches will be used? Of the many different models and approaches that could be developed what methods will be used and, maybe more importantly, which ones won't be used? This step could be answered by a brain-storming session of the many different ways to reach the objective with the risks, assumptions, and probability of success defined for each approach. Sometimes you may want to develop competing models and see how the results compare or do some type of Bayesian model averaging to gain a composite model.

- What does a successful solution look like? After defining the set of modeling approaches, and weighing the pros and cons of each approach, the team needs to agree upon what is a successful solution. I am not saying the team needs to agree upon the best solution or the optimal solution. There may not be one. Instead the team needs to decide, in advance, the criteria for an *acceptable* solution, e.g., the model will have the smallest sum of squares residual or Akaike Information Criteria (AIC), no estimable parameter will have a relative standard error exceeding 50%, no parameter will be unidentifiable, no observable bias in the goodness of fit plots, etc.

Every attempt should be made to make the criteria as quantifiable as possible. For example, the 50% criteria for parameter relative standard error is a hard, objective criteria, but the criteria of "no observable bias" in the goodness of fit plots is a soft criteria and qualifiers around that statement are recommended. This statement could be changed to "a Runs Test of the residuals is non-significant at p>0.05." Once the acceptance criteria is identified, the team can decide to weigh these criteria in terms of importance. For example, it may be more important to have no bias in the model but to maybe accept a model with larger AIC. Are any criteria "a must have?" For example, parameter identifiability is often a "must have" of any solution. If the problem consists of multiple objectives, there may be multiple sets of independent criteria.

Once the solutions are identified, the team should ask themselves the following questions: "Could we have done better?" "What are the consequences of our solution?" "Are we sure this will produce the result we need?" "Is this a marginal solution or a maximized solution?" The answer to some of these questions may cause the team to evaluate whether they need to pursue further modeling.

- What will be the organizational structure of the team? Everyone works differently. This question is meant to address differences in how people work when they work together. When and how often will the group meet to discuss the project? Regular meetings are a key to successful collaborations but don't overdo it. What will be the primary means of communication outside of real-time meetings? What are the roles and responsibilities of each team member? Do you have the right team members for success? Are others needed? Who will facilitate team discussions? Who will write the team minutes?

Hopefully, by addressing issues that arise during the Storming/Norming stage, the team can progress to the Performing stage. Some teams, however, remain stuck, never reaching the Performing stage. To overcome the inability of a team to agree on things, the "Six Thinking Hats" concept may be helpful. People come to teams having different perspectives, or different hats as Edwin de Bono (1985) says. Some people are fact-driven and look only at what is presented in front of them (they wear white hats). Some use their gut and rely on intuition to make a decision (they wear red hats). Some are naturally pessimists, look at the down-side of decisions, and are cautious decision-makers (they wear black hats). Others are more creative in their decision-making and less skeptical of ideas (they wear green hats). Others are naturally optimists and look for the up-side of decisions and ideas (they wear yellow hats).

When you come to a meeting, people may wear different hats and as the meeting progresses they may switch to wearing other hats. This leads to divergent, ineffective thinking that hinders group consensus and team building. De Bono argues that people need to align their hats to create what he calls "parallel thinking." First they may put on the white hat and look only at the facts to put everyone at the same place. When wearing the white hat, opinions and beliefs should be put aside. Then, they may put on the green hat and get creative about solutions. The group may then put on the yellow and black hats looking for the upside and downside of solutions. The red hat may be called into play afterwards to allow people to voice their opinions about particular solutions. The idea is to have everyone on the team wear a single hat for a limited period of time forcing people to focus their energy and attention in one direction.

To facilitate this process, de Bono recommends that a neutral facilitator wears what he calls a blue hat and controls the process so that everyone else can wear the same hat and follow the guidelines. The advantages of the method are that it eliminates rank and individual egos within a group since everyone is focusing on one direction and forces everyone to look at all sides of a problem and possible solutions before forming a consensus.

How might the Six Thinking Hats look in practice? As an example, let's examine model development in anticancer research. Pharmacologists will implant tumors into immune-impaired mice (this is called a xenograft model), allow the tumors to grow to a fixed size, and then administer a potential new anticancer drug to see whether the tumor shrinks in size, stays the same, or continues to grow. Although scientists have gotten very good at curing cancer in mice, they have not been so good at translating these results to humans. One difficulty is scaling the dose causing tumor shrinkage in mice to a pharmacologically equivalent dose in humans.

Suppose a pharmacologist (P), oncologist (O), and modeler (M) were tasked with developing a mathematical model of tumor growth in mice following treatment with a new anticancer drug and to predict what the efficacious dose in humans would be. First, it's interesting to see what a meeting might look like without using the Six Thinking Hats. It might go something like this:

P: "I've looked at the data and it looks like a Gompertz model will fit it."

M: "A Gompertz model is too empirical. It'll be difficult to extrapolate to humans. We should use a mechanistic model."

O: "I don't understand why we even need a model. The efficacious dose was 2 mg/kg [in mice], why don't we give a dose of about 150 mg to humans?"

P: "You can't just use the same dose as in mice."

O: "Why not? It's a protein. Proteins scale linearly across species."

M: "But what if we need to dose twice-a-day in humans, or once weekly, how would we extrapolate that? Is it half the dose or seven times the dose? No, we need a mechanistic model for this task."

As you can see in this scenario, ideas are floated up and then shot down. The upside to any idea is never really examined. This could go round and round with agreement on how best to proceed maybe never being achieved. Now let's look at how this conversation might go using the Six Thinking Hats:

M: "I've invited Steve here today to act as a facilitator for us. Steve, take it away."

Steve: "Hi. What I would like for you to do is to first identify what are our options."

M: "We can use a mechanistic model."

P: "Whatever model we choose it needs to be consistent with other models of tumor growth. We should use the Gompertz model."

M: "The Gompertz model is empirical. We can't easily translate them to humans."

Steve: "Right now we're only focusing on our options. We're not looking to veto options."

M: "If that's the case then we should also consider agent-based models."

O: "I don't know about which model we should use, but this drug is a protein and proteins scale linearly across species with regards to dose. We could just give the equivalent dose in humans on a mg/kg basis."

Steve: "Let's explore this last issue. What are the positives and negatives to scaling the dose?"

P: "Extrapolation would be easily explained to people."

M: "It doesn't help us if we need to use a dosing regimen that is different than the once-daily dosing regimen used in the xenograft studies. What if we need a once-weekly regimen? Do we multiply the daily dose by seven?"

O: "If we did that, then we might get too many adverse events in humans."

Steve: "So it sounds like scaling is not a viable solution. Let's go back to a proposal from earlier. Are there any objections to us focusing on mechanistic models as a solution for the moment? What other upsides are there to using a mechanistic model?"

M: "It allows us to simulate different dosing regimens."

P: "Mechanistic models try to model the physiology of tumor growth. It'll be easier for me to explain it to my colleagues."

O: "I agree."

Steve: "What are the downsides to these models?"

P: "They're hard to explain and they can't account for every little detail. Cancer is too complicated."

M: "There may be many model parameters that we have to estimate. Some of them may be unidentifiable."

Steve: "But what about the Gompertz model that was recommended?"

P: "There is a long history of its use in modeling xenograft data."

M: "Yes, but there is no easy way to scale them to humans. We can't translate them."

O: "If we can't translate them, why would we use them?"

Notice how the facilitator focuses the conversation on just one aspect of discussion. Instead of a free-for-all conversation with everyone offering ideas, debating results, and stating opinions, the conversation is centered on one area thereby improving group dynamics and allowing everyone to get their turn. As the facilitator rotates through the hats, parallel thinking is used to try to find a solution or strategy to which everyone agrees. Instead of having everyone being adversarial, with the Six Thinking Hats there is cooperative exploration of a topic.

Returning back to the Tuckman model, after the Storming/Norming stage is the Performing stage in which the team knows what it is doing and how to do it. Members take ownership of the process and outcome. If the team members don't really care about the outcome, their participation will be half-hearted which could lead to resentment from other team members. All members have a shared vision to reach the goal. There is a rapport among team members and although there may be disagreements in the team, these differences are worked out without leading to long-term resentment and team dysfunction. Team loyalty and functioning remain high at this stage, but changes to the team at this stage may move them back into the Storming/Norming stage.

The last stage, the Adjourning stage was not part of the original Tuckman model, but was added later. This stage is sometimes called the mourning stage because this is when the team objectives have been achieved and the team disbands.

A few comments need to be made regarding the Tuckman model. First, some stages of the model may never be reached. Some teams may switch back and forth between stages and for some teams stages may overlap. Figure 10 is a modification of the Tuckman model taking into account overlap of stages and movement back and forth between stages. Although Tuckman's theory has been criticized for over-generalizing how groups interact and perform (the same can be said of almost any model) and that the model assumes that teams move through stages in a predictable manner, my personal experience has been that the Tuckman model does a pretty good job of explaining how teams evolve over time.

Defining goals and expectations in the Storming/Norming stage are just some of the internal factors needed for collaborative success. There are also external factors that play a role. Teams must have sufficient resources, staff, and time to complete the mission, as well as a strong, organized leader who acts impartially to help guide the group to success. Lack of any of these puts the completion of the entire project into jeopardy.

Another major external factor for a successful collaboration is an appropriate working environment that encourages collaboration (Mattessich et al., 2001). Companies that have a history of, or encourage collaboration, among employees, teams, and divisions will be more likely to succeed than those that do not. Have you ever heard of the Sony iPod? Of course not. However, you've probably heard of the Sony Walkman and Diskman. Before there were MP3 players everywhere, Sony dominated the market. Sony was the proverbial 10,000 pound gorilla on the block, and Apple was just an upstart. Sony should have been able to build an iPod equivalent MP3 player and then destroy Apple. Sony had Sony Music, Sony Electronics, Sony's distribution network, and they even made the batteries for Apple's iPod. Why didn't Sony come to dominate the MP3 market like Apple? As Morton Hansen (2009) explains, Sony's highly competitive culture didn't allow for effective collaboration. It didn't allow for everyone to share in the glory. So Apple beat Sony to market, launched iTunes as a way to distribute music, and now Apple is the 10,000 pound gorilla.

Collaborative teams need an effective way to openly and frequently communicate with each other; the earlier in the process the better. The importance of this cannot be over-emphasized. The role of the team leader is critical to make sure everyone has their say and to encourage those who might not readily voice an opinion to feel safe enough to speak their mind. Communications must be inclusive among all team members because communication with only some of the team members may lead to a splintered group.

Collaboration can be done in a synchronous, asynchronous, or mixed manner. In synchronous collaboration (SC) the collaborators can work together in a real-time manner to exchange ideas, discuss, and react to the ideas of others. In an asynchronous collaboration (ASC) collaborators are often in different geographical locales and/or in different time zones such that the exchange of ideas cannot be in real time among individuals. Collaboration requires tools that allow individuals to communicate. To maximize SC, in the absence of face-to-face meetings, communications by telephone, internet like WebEx or Skype, or videoconferencing should be used. If all individuals can work on the model and have access to it, some way to keep track of changes made to the model by different individuals (version control) is needed.

Collaborative teams that are at the same site and work at the same time have obvious advantages, but it is still an effort to get face-to-face time with people. People are busy. Very few of us actually just walk over and talk to people anymore when we have a problem or question. We email, instant message them, or call them on the phone. Allen (1977) studied the amount of communication between engineers as a function of the distance between them and found that communication exponentially decreased as the distance between the engineers increased, an effect coined as the 'Allen curve.' Subjects were 10-times more likely to talk to the person at the desk next to them than someone who was 150 feet away. At 30 feet distance, there was only an 8% chance of personally communicating with someone once a week. It's the whole 'out of sight, out of mind' phenomenon.

Even though these studies were done 40 years ago, before the internet, email, cell phones, and teleconferences, Allen and Henn (2006) argue that the curve still applies today. Therefore, it's important to actively work to overcome the inertia for face-to-face communication. One thing that might help is to have a social component to the team where team members meet face-to-face outside the project to discuss things other than work. This helps to build trust, form stronger relationships between the team members, and works against the Allen curve.

In ASC, the team is virtual and there is minimal personal interaction, face-to-face contact, and verbal communication. Communication will be harder to achieve with ACS because of time differences and potential language differences. Webpages, electronic notebooks, or note boards are needed to post information to the other team members. Such methods may need to be designed in multiple languages to accommodate all team members from different countries. ASC is not as efficient as SC but does have the advantage that it can allow individuals the time to understand changes to the model and its impact. For instance, a modeler may be able to modify a model, store it on an access site, and then, when the other parts of the team arrive for work later they can review the work that was done earlier by the modeler.

With today's work environment, a mix of SC and ASC is the norm. Teams may work face-to-face at times during the day, but, then may communicate with each other in an asynchronous virtual manner at other times. For instance, there may be daily team meetings with updates on the project but thereafter team members communicate by email. This requires that the tools for both SC and ASC be provided to team members for successful communication.

In leaving this topic, even with understanding how teams behave over time, collaboration is not always easy. Have you ever sat and watched kids play together? Did you notice how easy it was for all of them to come together and play? How, if there is a common goal, it was natural for each of them to rally around the others to reach that goal. How they called out those who weren't meeting group expectations. What happens to us as we grow up that, as adults, we can't form groups so easily anymore? I think part of what happens is that, as adults, we view collaboration as work. Remember the team project in high school or college where you had to work with others as part of a project for your grade? Didn't it always seem there was someone who didn't carry their workload and rode on the other's backs for the grade? We remember that and are hesitant to fully participate in collaborative projects. It doesn't have to be that way. The reason that kids work so well together is that they collaborate to have fun. Indeed, collaboration can and should be fun, not a soul-crunching grind. Collaboration when done properly is a social event where team members enjoy getting together to solve problems, to work (and yes it may be hard work), and to have fun.

– Five –
Preparation is the Key to Success

You've been working to establish trust and credibility at your job. You are collaborating on the model and you have the results of the analysis. Now you need to present those results to an audience. Most modelers I know spend days, weeks, sometimes months, analyzing data, but then spend a tiny fraction of that time, maybe just a couple of hours, working on their presentation. Slides are haphazardly put together. No time is spent practicing; their message tends to get lost in minutiae and a chaotic storyline. When an audience doesn't understand the model, modelers often blame the audience ("they just don't get it") rather than themselves.

No matter how good the science, no matter how useful the model, without a successful presentation, the audience won't buy it. They won't understand it. They'll be bored or lost. We've all been to presentations like these. Mind-numbing. Confusing. Rambling. They've been called "Death by PowerPoint" (coined by Angela Garber in 2001), "PowerPoint Poisoning" (coined by Scott Adams, the creator of Dilbert in 2000), and "PowerPointlessness" (coined by James MacKenzie in 2000). We mock these presentations, but accept them as a fact of life. Boring is the new normal.

Being prepared is an important life skill – like the Boy Scouts of America motto says, "Be Prepared." And yet most modelers fail to adequately prepare for important presentations. Alexander Graham Bell once said that "Before anything else, preparation is the key to success." Useful words. Hence, the title of the chapter. This chapter will walk you through the elements of preparing for a successful presentation, while the next chapter will deal with how to give that presentation to an audience.

Know Your Audience

With today's software it's easy to jump right in and start making slides for your presentation. Many people do just that. However, to truly connect with your audience, you have to know who your audience is. The presentation you prepare for a peer group of modelers will be different from the presentation you prepare for a nontechnical audience. Heaven help you if you present the same material to both groups. Presenting technical material to a nontechnical audience will overwhelm them, while presenting a nontechnical talk to a peer group will leave them bored and under-impressed.

You can start to analyze your audience by asking yourself who, what, where, when, how, and why?

- **To whom are you presenting?** This is a very broad question and there are many aspects that need to be addressed. What is the size of the group? Where are they from? Do you know them? Do they trust you? Are you a credible presenter to them? Each of these questions will cause you to vary your material and how you present it.

  Are you presenting to a large group, a small group, or to just one person? Is that one person your boss? You wouldn't give the same presentation to a large group as you would to a small group. Well, maybe you would, but that would be a mistake. Large audiences are less personal and tend to be more formal, usually on a stage or behind a podium. Smaller audiences are more intimate and conversational. People can interrupt you during your talk. With a large group, you wouldn't expect such interruptions. There may not even be questions afterwards. With one person you can tailor the message completely to that person and you can expect the presentation to be more conversational with frequent interruptions and questions.

What is the audience's level of technical expertise or knowledge of the subject? Are they subject-matter experts? Knowing the technical level of the audience will affect how scientific and technical your presentation is. Try to be as specific as you can be when you explore the level of knowledge of your audience to better tailor your message. For example, presenting the results of your Bayesian analysis to a group of statisticians may appear, on its face, that you could gloss over background about Bayes Theorem, but what if the audience was a group of frequentists? Then you may need to devote time in your presentation to remind them of the basic principles of Bayesian statistics like choice of priors, etc. Failure to do so may result in the audience being confused because they do not understand your methods.

Do you know the audience personally or are they strangers? How you present will be different if you personally know your audience than if you've never met. Some people say they present better in front of strangers because if they bomb they don't really know anyone in the audience anyway. Others say they hate speaking in front of strangers for that very reason - because they don't know anyone in the audience. Think about who you are more comfortable speaking to and, if you are speaking to a group you are uncomfortable with, practice more to get over your nerves.

What is your level of trust and credibility in the audience? If you are an unknown quantity to the audience then you need to rapidly establish trust and credibility with them. If the audience knows you then you need to maintain and build on their confidence. The chapter on Trust and Credibility earlier in the book discusses this in detail.

Is your boss in the audience? I don't know about you, but even after as many presentations as I have given, I still am especially nervous when my boss is in the audience. I rationalize as much as I can but it still happens. Related to this is when a single person in the audience is responsible for decision making. That is the person to whom you need to tailor your presentation. This will be discussed in the section on Taming Your Hippo.

Are there cultural differences of which you should be aware? Whether the audience is of a different ethnicity or whether there are cultural differences between you and the audience may affect your presentation. I work for a Japanese company. I frequently have team members living in Japan who listen to me on the phone or via WebEx when I give a presentation. I have to be careful to talk a little bit slower with longer pauses between sentences to allow for translation. I also have to make sure I don't use U.S.-specific idioms or slang they might not understand. When I speak in person to audiences from different countries, I need to carefully gauge my eye contact, level of emotion, and body language so my message is not misconstrued. In some societies, a high level of emotion is a good thing (like the United States and China), but in others it's not (like in Japan). Even something like a number could be misunderstood. For instance, a billion in the U.S. means a thousand million but not too long ago in the United Kingdom it meant a million millions.

Are there sex differences of which you need to be aware? As we all know, men and women are simply different and they respond differently to presentations. For example, during a presentation, men will nod their heads when they are in agreement with something that was just said. Women tend to nod their heads to show they are listening to you. It doesn't mean they necessarily agree with you. Conversely, if a woman is speaking and she doesn't see you nod as she is speaking, she's going to think you either don't agree or aren't listening. This simple thing can be a source of confusion and anger between the sexes.

Are there age differences of which you need to be aware? It would be a mistake to reference something the audience would not understand. For instance, I'm almost 50 years old. I have as, a reference point, computer software and hardware going all the way back to the 1970's. I played Pong when it first came out. My first use of a computer was through a teletype. I am a dinosaur. Today, I work with adults who are in their early 30s. They've never seen a teletype and they might have heard of Pong if they are real computer nerds. In my talks, if I made reference to when I used to analyze data on my 386 computer or do hand calculations on my TI-55 calculator, neither reference would be understood by my 30 year old colleagues. You need to make certain your references are consistent with the age of the audience and if you do reference something you think they may not know about, make sure you explain it.

- **What is the audience's mood, attitudes, and beliefs?** This can't really be assessed until right before the presentation but it's easy to see you will have a greater chance of reaching your goal if the audience is in a good mood. If you have to present after a speaker who was terrible, that negative audience energy will carry over to you, and you may have a much higher hurdle to reach your goal.

Analyzing the audience's attitudes and beliefs is also important. An attitude is what a person likes or dislikes while a belief is something they think is true or false. If the audience in general agrees with you, or your ideas, then it will be easier to reach your goal. If you know up front your audience won't agree with your ideas, you need to form a much greater emotional bond with them before they will consider your ideas. If you know the audience agrees with your ideas in general then you can build on those ideas to maximize reaching your goal.

- **Where will you be presenting?** Where you present will affect both you and your audience. Will you be presenting in person or virtually? If I am presenting personally, what is the room like? I went to a conference once where I was the keynote speaker and the stage was right behind this big column in the center of the room. Like a dummy I went back and forth across the stage during my presentation so I could see and talk to both sides of the audience. What I should have done was stepped off the stage and spoke to the audience in front of the column. Problem solved and it would have really showed that I cared about the audience by doing so. The room you present in is not just a room; it's the setting for what you have to say. A room that is too hot. A room that has uncomfortable seating. A room with a big column right in front of the speaker. All kinds of little details can kill an otherwise great presentation. If you can, go to the room beforehand. Sit in a few seats around the room. How do things look? How do they sound? Are there things that need to be fixed before you start? Anything you can do to improve things from the audience's perspective will improve the audience's reception to your presentation.

How large is the audience? Will it be in an auditorium or a conference room? It may sound strange but presentations can be intimate or they can anthem-size. For example, if you are presenting in an auditorium, then your slides need to be created in a large font size so that everyone in the room can read them. If you are presenting in a conference room you can get by with smaller font sizes and, in fact, using a large font size will not be appreciated in this setting. The size of the room will also affect how you give your presentation. Big rooms require big gestures. Go watch any TED talk (http://www.ted.com/talks) and you will know what I mean by an anthem-size talk.

Will all the attendees be in the room with me or will some people be on the phone via teleconference or by videoconference? Presenting when everyone is in the same room is different than when you present and some people are in the room and some people are on the phone. What tends to happen when someone is on the phone is that the needs of the few (the people on the phone) outweigh the needs of the many (the room). How many times have you been in a presentation with a room full of people discussing a topic and suddenly the voice on the phone interrupts and says "I can't hear the question. Can you speak into the microphone?" Everything stops. The microphone gets moved around, the flow of the conversation is halted, and then the dynamic of the conversation tries to get started again. Videoconferences also present challenges, often technological in nature. Videos freeze. Time is spent trying to get it going again. This eats into your presentation time. Some of these challenges cannot be overcome but some can, such as making sure there is an even disbursement of microphones around a conference table prior to the start of the presentation or making sure there is enough time for you to ensure things are working prior to your presentation.

- **When will you be presenting?** It may seem obvious, but know what time you are speaking. Don't be late. The negative effects of being late may seem evident but let me state them for you: it undermines your credibility, you have less time to speak, you irritate the audience, you may not be able to speak as other speakers are brought in to take your place, and the list goes on and on. So, don't be late.

Are you the sole speaker, or one of a group of speakers? If you are part of a group, are you the first, middle, or last speaker? If you are part of a group of speakers you may be presenting on similar material. If you are the first speaker, you set the tone for everyone else. Failure here may cause audience members to choose to leave. If you are speaking last you must ensure you are not covering material already presented by other speakers. Make sure your material is unique and not repetitive.

Are you presenting in the morning when people are still trying to wake up? If so, you need to make sure your energy level is sufficient to wake them up. If you are the speaker just before lunch, your audience is going to be antsy to get out of there and eat. If you are the first speaker after lunch, your audience may start to get the early afternoon dropsy from their insulin kicking in and dropping their blood glucose concentrations. If you are the last speaker, people may be ready to go home for the day, but at least you are in the enviable position in that people tend to remember the last speaker of the day more than the speakers in the middle of the day.

So when is the best time of day to give a presentation? I prefer midmorning around 10:00 or 10:30 am. By midmorning, people have woken up and are not quite hungry for lunch. The day is still early enough that they aren't starting to think about going home. What is the best day of the week to be presenting? A 2008 survey by Accountemps has suggested that Tuesday is the best. Tuesday tends to be the busiest day of the week, people are in the full swing of work, aren't depressed about being at work on Monday, and aren't yet thinking of the weekend.

- **How will your presentation be given?** Do you want to give your presentation using slides or just talk to the audience? In today's business world where slides are ubiquitous and used even for the most mundane meetings, it seems heretical but you don't always need to use slides. You can just talk. It's been argued that the use

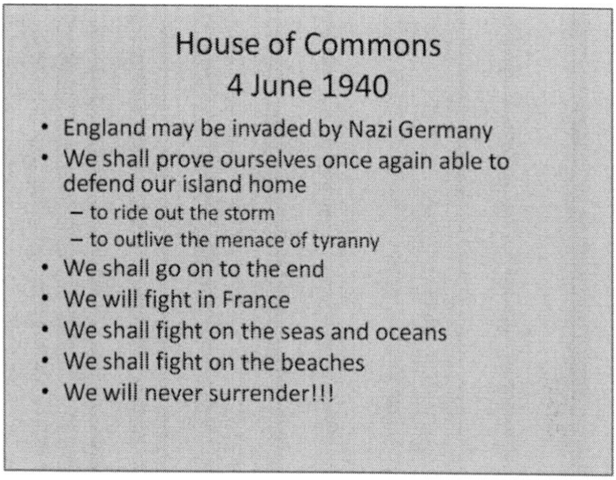

Figure 11. Not every presentation needs to use slides. Imagine if Winston Churchill's 1940 "We Shall Fight Them on the Beaches" speech was done using PowerPoint.

of PowerPoint has dumbed down our ability to communicate and fails to create that emotional resonance needed to move an audience.

Taking a cue from Jon Steel's book *Perfect Pitch* (2007), think of Martin Luther King's "I Have a Dream" speech, Abraham Lincoln's Gettysburg Address, or Winston Churchill's "We Shall Fight Them on the Beaches" speech. Imagine if these had been given using PowerPoint (Figure 11). These great speeches would lose their impact. There would be no connection with the audience. Using a poorly prepared slide deck or an inappropriate slide deck can actually be a barrier to what you want to accomplish. For most scientific presentations, however, it would be difficult to present data without a slide deck, but for presentations like keynote addresses this is a viable option.

Are you giving a virtual presentation? Virtual presentations are a different beast entirely from in-person presentations. The audience doesn't see you. You are this disembodied voice and all they have to see are your slides. This makes for some unique challenges both to the audience and to you. More will be discussed on this topic later in the book.

How long do you have to present? You don't want to present an hour long presentation when you only have 10 minutes and vice-versa. The less time you have to present the more tailored and distinct the presentation needs to be. There is a rule of presentations – NEVER steal your audience's time. If you have 15 minutes, you had better not go over your time limit unless you speak like Mahatma Gandhi or Winston Churchill. Don't be the guy who speed talks to cover a longer presentation in a shorter period of time. Stealing your audience's time is rude and disrespectful. You are not considering their needs and are thinking only of yourself.

- **Why is the audience there?** This may, perhaps, be the most important question to answer because, if you know why the audience is there, you can tailor your material to meet their needs. If they are there to learn something new, you can make your talk more educational without so much as an agenda other than teaching a new topic. If they are there to learn the results of your analysis, focus on the results and not so much on the methods. I've seen many modeling presentations derailed by the presenter spending too much time on the model and not enough time on the results and conclusions.

Every one of these questions will help you tailor your message and presentation. It's important for you to learn to become audience-centered, instead of speaker-centered, as you prepare your presentation. Most speakers tend to prepare their slides based on what they think should be covered in the presentation, which is not necessarily what the audience needs to have covered to understand and buy it. By thinking of the needs of

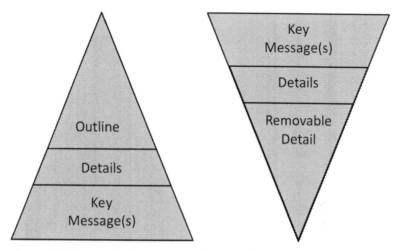

Figure 12. Most scientists present their results using a pyramid design (left) where details are presented prior to their key message(s). It is better to use an inverted pyramid design (right) where the main message is presented up-front followed by essential supporting details and then nonessential removable details that if omitted do not result in loss of clarity regarding the key message(s).

the audience, you are already starting to connect to them. Thinking of the audience will also help you find your common ground, the material necessary to establish a connection with your audience.

What Is Your Key Message?

Presentations need to be laser focused and that focus starts with the key message (Figure 12). Its been said that 24 hours after your presentation, the audience will forget 75% of your material. Ask yourself, if the audience remembers only one thing, what is the one thing you want them to remember? That is your key message. It needs to be concise, clear, and to the point. Write it down. If it needs punctuation or if you need to pause for a breath it may be too long and will need to be shortened. Often the key message is not the model itself, it's what the model provides. What are the model's benefits? What are its insights?

Example messages might be:

- Sales will increase 20% next year to 120 million dollars based predominantly from increased sales of Drug X.

- This company is in trouble. Sales will be down two billion dollars next year with the patent loss of Drug X.

- Fifty mg is the dose needed to decrease cholesterol by at least 20 mg/dL with 90% confidence.

- This model effectively integrates systems biology, preclinical pharmacology, and clinical results allowing us to form a platform for future drug discovery.

It's important to clearly state your message. Notice how the sample messages were explicit and simple. You might think that after your brilliant presentation that everyone will get your message, but you would be surprised. An audience that isn't explicitly given the message forms their own message, which may not be the one you want them to remember.

As you prepare to write your message, think about the audience. Does it have some kind of hook the audience will remember? Will the audience care about the message? Does your message help the audience? Does it address the benefits of the model? If some action is desired of the audience afterwards, does the message lead the audience towards the action? These questions should help you write the message, then once you've written it, get out your editing pen and shorten it. Take a step back and reflect. Is this the one thing I want the audience to know?

What Are the Secondary Points?

After you have identified your key message, what are the other important secondary points you want to deliver? No more than two or three secondary points should be presented and each of these points should support the key message. You don't want a secondary point that is discordant from the key message, since that might lead to questions and uncertainties regarding the key message. For instance, suppose your projections indicate sales will increase 20% next year due to increased sales of Drug X. Your secondary points might be that a disproportionate percentage of that increase is due to European sales because of early regulatory approval compared to the rest of world, that the projection assumes that sales trends for your largest competitor holding constant during the next year, and that drug approval for a me-too product being developed by another company is delayed for two years. If your key message was that a 50 mg dose is needed to decrease cholesterol by at least 20 mg/dL with 90% confidence, your secondary points might be that HDL and LDL cholesterol is expected to remain constant, elderly patients may need a dose of 25 mg due to decreased kidney elimination in that population, and that this recommendation assumes the population for which the model was built upon generalizes to the population that will be used to gain regulatory approval. You wouldn't want to have as a secondary message something to the effect of "a dose of 75 mg/dL will decrease cholesterol by 30 mg/dL with the same level of confidence" because then it appears that you are recommending both 50 and 75 mg. The 75 mg dose statement muddies the clarity of your key recommendation.

As you put together your key message and supporting points think about it from the audience's perspective. Be audience-centric. If you were in the audience what would you want to know? Is it the model? The data used to build the model? The assumptions of the model? The limitations of the model? Or its conclusions and predictions? Anyone can present a table of parameter estimates or p-values, but it takes real skill to be able to present and interpret those results to a nontechnical audience in a manner they comprehend with an appreciative understanding of its assumptions and limitations. That's what separates the average from the model communicators.

Supporting Data

Now that you have identified your key message and your secondary points, what data are you going to present to support those points? For each of your key and secondary points you need to identify the material that will be used to support them. Returning to the cholesterol example, the supporting data could be:

a) 50 mg dose (key point):

b) Regression analysis supports a linear relationship between steady-state drug concentrations and decreased cholesterol.

c) A steady-state concentration of 100 ng/mL is needed to produce no less than 20 mg/dL decrease in cholesterol with 90% confidence.

d) The dose that produces a steady-state concentration of at least 100 ng/mL in 90% of subjects is 50 mg.

2) HDL and LDL cholesterol is expected to remain constant (1st secondary point).

a) Regression analysis failed to detect any relationship between drug concentrations and either HDL or LDL cholesterol.

b) No evidence of hysteresis was present.

c) No other drugs in this class have HDL or LDL effects.

3) Elderly patients may require a dose of 25 mg because of decreased kidney elimination in that population (2nd secondary point).

a) Analysis of the concentration-time profiles in elderly patients have drug concentrations almost twice that of younger adults.

b) The drug is removed from the body almost entirely by the kidney and renal function decreases as you get older such that an 85 year old has half the renal function of a 20 year old.

4) This recommendation assumes that the population the model was built upon generalizes to the treatable population.

a) There is no reason to suspect that there will be any pharmacokinetic differences between populations since they are both expected to have similar renal function.

b) There are some risks in the assumption that the drug's effects will be the same between the populations since the treatable population will have access to a wider list of concomitantly prescribed medications that may interfere with the drug's efficacy and patients in the treatable population will have higher baseline cholesterol than the model building population.

Notice how the model was only peripherally used to support the secondary points. As you present the first supporting point you have the option of presenting the model in greater detail at that time, waiting until you finish your supporting points, or not presenting the model at all unless someone asks. The question of whether to present the model or not depends upon audience expectations. It may be expected that the model is presented to support your conclusions or it may not be necessary if the audience is really only interested in your recommendation.

Organizing Your Material

Many people when they prepare for a presentation create the slide deck on the fly. They have a general idea of what they want to say but it's not very focused. Consequently, it's a lot like Billy in the Family Circus comic (Figure 13). Shown in the figure, his mother asks him to walk a letter to the mailbox outside. As he goes from his kitchen to the mailbox, instead of going straight to the mailbox, he goes here, he goes there, and he stops to pet the dog. He eventually gets to the mailbox but it's in this crazy, curvy path with many stops along the way. A lot of scientific presentations are like Billy – they go every which way. Main points are buried. Superfluous ideas are presented. Text is added to slides that is not needed. Graphs are added because they look cool. There are awkward transitions. It's all very haphazard. And not until the end are high level messages and conclusions

Figure 13. Instead of using the most direct route from going to Point A to Point B in a presentation, many speakers take side-journeys and excursions that distract from the message. They stop and present material that doesn't increase clarity and they dwell on material that might be redundant, just like Billy in the Family Circus. © *FAMILY CIRCUS (2012) Bil Keane, Inc. King Features Syndicate.*

presented, as if the presentation were a murder mystery where the murderer is announced by the detective at the end of the book.

Organizing your material will help you keep a laser focus on what's important and will allow you to cohesively build your arguments to support your key message without distractions and getting caught up in minutiae. Dave Paradi in his book *Present So They Get It* (2012) uses the metaphor of a GPS for the outline. By knowing your starting point and your destination you can lay out the map where you need the audience to go. Like a GPS, where you can choose to take the fastest route or the most direct route, with your presentation you can choose to take the most straightforward route, a leisurely route, or a route that makes important stops along the way.

The general organization of your presentation should follow key messages, introduction, body of talk, and conclusions. In an audience-centric presentation, the material is organized to help the audience remember the key ideas. As stated many times in this book, plan and state your key message first, along with a few key pieces of supporting evidence. If you give the conclusions up-front it will get the audience interested in how you got there, it tells them why they should listen to you, and, if they aren't interested, at least they know what the final message is. There is also one added benefit. How many times have you had to give a presentation but the presenters before you ran over their time limit leaving you with a fraction of your original time to make your point? By presenting your conclusions up front you get right to the point. Then, if people want to follow up with you later for details they can.

After you make your main points and you move into the body of the talk, there are lots of different styles you can use to organize your material. You could of course use the key message-supporting point format, where each supporting point represents a module of slides all of which support the key message. Another style is the classic scientific method where you present the background, methods, results, and then conclusions. Most scientists are familiar with this style. There are other styles as well. The Problem-Solution approach is to present the problem, present your proposal to solve the problem, present how you will test your proposal as a solution to the problem, show your results, present what conclusions can be drawn, and conclude by suggesting future analyses. Of the two, I prefer the Problem-Solution approach because most of the projects I am on have a goal of solving some problem. The teams I work with are interested in a solution to a problem. Being explicit in what is the problem and what is the solution keeps the team on track. The Scientific Method style is kind of old fashioned and the team has to wait till the end for a conclusion (essentially it is the murder mystery approach). Another style is the chronological style: present the past, the present, and then the future. This type of presentation may be useful if you are trying to teach new methods to an audience.

Whatever style you choose remember this, your presentation is not a paper. Most scientists go with the Scientific method approach because it follows the format of a paper: introduction, methods, results, etc. This makes for a

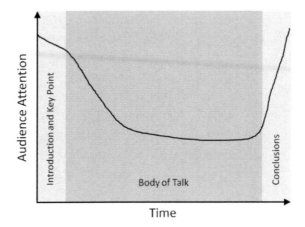

Figure 14. An audience's attention is highest at the beginning and end of your talk. During the body of your talk is when your audience's attention is at its lowest. As you prepare your material you need to find ways to keep their attention. *Redrawn and modified from Reimold and Reimold, 2003.*

highly structured talk that follows a familiar pattern. If you want to shake things up and get your audience's attention, think outside the familiar pattern and use a style that they might not be used to seeing. Use a style that best fits what you are trying to convey.

Which outline style you choose depends on your goal and your audience. Which style will best convey your main ideas? Which style would be the most logical to the audience? Which style would be the easiest for them to understand the material? As you prepare your talk, think about the audience's point of view, their attention span, and how much information they can comprehend and retain at one sitting. Figure 14 shows audience attention over time (Reimold and Reimold, 2003). Their attention is at its highest during your introduction and as you state the key message. They are excited by the unknown and what you might have to say. As you start to present their attention wanes and is at its lowest during the body of your talk, the point when you presenting the details. When you get to your conclusions, their attention starts to rise again. As a presenter, you may not want to put really difficult material near the end of your talk, when attention is at its lowest. Moving it towards early in the presentation may allow the audience to understand it better.

Having chosen a style, many people sit down at a computer and sketch out their presentation from scratch using PowerPoint, without much planning or forethought. There is nothing wrong with that, except that PowerPoint is a linear program. It forces you to move from Slide 1 to Slide 2 to Slide 3, etc., and it may be hard to visualize as you prepare how all the elements in the presentation will tie together, especially if your presentation is complex. In this case you may need other tools to help you plan. One method to plan your presentation, the old fashion way, is to use Sticky Notes to outline your presentation. After writing each idea or design element of the presentation on a Sticky Note you can then rearrange the ideas and topics so that the presentation has the flow you want to create. The flow of notes and ideas can then be translated to your presentation.

An alternative is to consider using mind-mapping software. A mind-map is a visual outline of information flows. Instead of bulleted, sequential formatting of information, mind-maps present a kind of spider web of information starting from a center point. They are meant to generalize and classify information and can help find gaps or presentation elements that might have been forgotten. Useful for brainstorming, they can be drawn by hand but there are a number of good commercial software packages available (SmartDraw, Mindjet, Mindgenius, XMind and MindMeister to name a few) and an open-source freeware program called Freemind. The difference between the commercial and open-source packages are the number of bells and whistles. Figure 15 presents a mind-map of the components of a presentation as discussed in this chapter drawn using Freemind. What is cool about a lot of these programs is that if you copy the map and then paste it into a Microsoft Word document, the entire mind-map shows up in bulleted outline form. The entire presentation leads up to your conclusions so don't underestimate their importance. They should be short and to the point. Restate your key message and the benefits to the audience. Stay focused on the message and don't try to introduce new

Figure 15. Example of a mind-map showing the questions you should ask yourself when preparing for a presentation.

material at this point as it will confuse your audience. If your presentation was leading up to a call to action, such as additional funds to continue your research or implementation of your results in future projects, now is the time to call for it. A strong conclusion is often the last thing the audience remembers, so make it count.

Slide Deck Do's and Don'ts

It's easy to make bad slides. People do it all the time. Too many words. Garish colors. Figures that don't make sense. Tables with too many numbers. It's easy and we see it every day. Bad slides confuse people. Bad slides bore people. And bad slides kill people. That's right. Bad slides kill. You heard me say it. It has been argued that bad data visualization was a contributing factor in the explosion of the Space Shuttle Challenger in 1986 (Tufte, 1997) and that bad slides also contributed to the loss of the Space Shuttle Columbia (Tufte, 2011). NASA is apparently not the only government agency that creates dangerous slides, U.S. National Forces do as well (Figure 16). I guess there is some truth to the old saying: "Guns don't kill people. Bullets do" (get the pun?). The U.S. Government is not the only purveyor of bad slide decks, all you have to do is go to work and it won't be long, maybe a matter of hours, before you see a bad slide deck there.

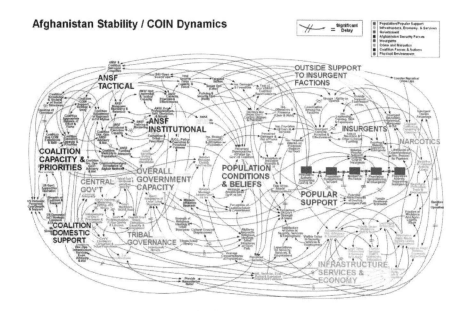

Figure 16. PowerPoint slide shown to U.S. commanders in Afghanistan showing the relationship between U.S. Forces, Afghan National Security Forces (dark blue), and the enemy (red). When shown this slide, Gen. Stanley Chrystal remarked "When we understand that slide, we'll have won the war." *Source: The New York Times (Bumiller, 4-26-2010).*

It would be simple for me, at this point, to present more examples of bad slides or bad graphs, ones that we could all laugh at (see http://www.statisticshowto.com/misleading-graphs for example). We could say, "What a clown for presenting such a slide. What was he thinking?" Chances are that whatever slides I use as an example, at some point in your career you've probably made similar slides yourself. I know I have. Gee-whiz graphics like 3-D histograms and ribbon time-series graphs. Check. Flying bullet points across the screen. Check. Too many words on a slide. Check. Cool colors that don't have any meaning. Check. Too many numbers. Check. Mea Culpa. I've done them all.

A complicating issue is that many modelers I know seem to equate detail with success. They fill every slide with details, charts, text, facts, and statistics, as if to say to the audience "look how much work I've done." There is a limit to how much information people can absorb and when it's too much it leads to "cognitive overload" (Sweller, 1988). People just cannot remember anymore when their limit has been reached. Their brain can't handle it and they stop paying attention. A classic example is the principle that people can retain only "7-chunks" of information in their short-term memory at any one time, which is the reason why telephone numbers are 7-digits in length. It probably won't take long for you to think back to a presentation where the presenter overloaded you with details to the point where you couldn't wait to escape. It may seem obvious but you don't want to overload your audience.

What can be done to rectify this sad situation? First, let's stop blaming the slide deck. It's not the slide deck's fault – it's our fault. When we make slides we tend to use the same formats and styles that we've used in the past. This has been referred to as Conway's Law (Harrison, 2010). If it's worked in the past, why change? Because audiences are unique and as such your presentation should be unique as well. Your presentation should be tailored to the audience, not a recycling of past slide decks with an update of the tables and figures. Conway's Law may be an issue when your company forces you to use their "corporate template." In that case you may need to just grin and bear it. Second, decide that your audience deserves the best and have your slide deck follow the 5 C's: consistent, clear, concise, cultured, and content. Each of these will be discussed in turn.

Consistent. Your slide deck should have a consistent background, format, layout, font, and graph style because inconsistency is the hallmark of sloppiness. Microsoft PowerPoint has a number of nice and pretty themes that you can choose from. Pick one and stay with it. If you need to make changes, create your own slide master so consistency is maintained across slides. Within a slide, regardless of where it is on the slide, increasing the font size, changing the color, or changing the font of some piece of text implies that what is changed is more important than other elements on the slide. Similarly, changing a chart symbol within a slide implies that something is important. Only change the font, color, size, or symbol when something is important and needs to be highlighted.

Clear. Keep your slides clear in the sense that you don't clutter it up with ornamentation to make a point. For example, in most cases there is little reason to use a 3D-bar chart when a series of 2D-bar charts can be used with more impact. Anything that distracts from the main point of the graph should be avoided; Edward Tufte refers to this as "chartjunk" (Tufte, 2001). Also, don't make a wall of numbers like the table of parameter estimates shown in Figure 17. Nobody can read such a table in any reasonable period of time. Such a slide could be the entire slide deck for a single presentation. Instead, highlight the salient data from a table as shown in Figure 18. Which parameters are particularly important? Can you add some interpretation to the parameters that one might not otherwise take away from a table? Similarly, don't make a wall of text, or make your text so small that no one can read it. There is an urban legend of a presentation made entirely in 5-point font. Can you imagine what that was like for the audience?

Bullets are short for "bulletpoints" which are meant to be short phrases or sentences that are meant to convey the main point. When you fill a bullet up with text you defeat its purpose. When shown a slide full of text (which has been jokingly called a slideument, a cross between a slide and a document) the audience is going to read the text on the slide and not pay attention to what you are saying. Also, slideuments that are too long won't be read in their entirety. There is one case where it is okay to use a slideument and that is when your audience might not be native English speakers. It may be easier for them to read the slide than to translate what you are verbally saying. In most cases you should limit yourself to the number of bullets and sub-bullets per slide. There are lots of recommendations for how many bullets and how many words per bullet. No more than six bullets with six to eight words per slide or less than five bullets per slide. These rules are silly. Do what makes sense and be consistent in your choice.

Final Parameter Estimates

Submodel	Parameter	Value	SE	BSV (%)*
Cancer	Clearance (L/h)	40.7	8.07	68
	V2 (L)	12300	1860	30
Healthy Males	Clearance (L/h)	10.2	3.87	68
	V2 (L)	7110	2130	30
Induction Model	CL, max induction (L/h)	320	85.3	**
CL = CL(0) + CLmax*Time**n/(T50 + Time)**n	T50 (h)	46.4	17.6	88
	shape parameter (n)	6.40	1.76	**
Bioavailability Model	F1 Fmax	1	fixed	**
F = 1 -F1max* Dose/(Dose + F1D50)	F1 D50	128	39.4	**
	Food effect on F1	-0.360	0.119	
Absorption Model	Ka (Group 1) per h	1.77	0.431	145
	Lag Time (Group 2) h	0.821	0.0386	**
	Ka (Group 2) per h	0.361	0.0362	145
	Lag Time (Group 2) h	0	fixed	**
	Proportion of Subjects in Group 1	0.970	0.240	
Distribution Parameters	Q (L/h)	198	40.9	**
	V3 (L)	1830	679	141
V2 = TVV2*(WGT/75)**1	Weight on V2	1	fixed	
	V3 multiplier for Study 2	23.5	7.42	
Inter-Occasion Variability	Clearance			18
	V2			18
Residual Variance Model	Proportional Error			11
Observed = Predicted*exp(e1) + ε2	Additive error	0.168		
* denotes common variability for both cancer patients and healthy males				
** denotes variance too small to estimate				

Figure 17. Slide of a table of parameter estimates I once presented to a project team. This type of slide is a "wall of numbers." There is so much information and jargon on this slide that it is incomprehensible.

Pharmacokinetic Conclusions

- AUC decreased over time due to enzyme induction
- Cancer patients had 75% lower AUC than healthy volunteers
- Food decreased AUC by 36%
- The amount of drug absorbed decreased with increasing dose
- Extensive tissue distribution
- No difference in pharmacokinetics between males and females
- Large variability in pharmacokinetics across patients

Figure 18. Key conclusions from Figure 17.

Clear also refers to your models and equations. Any equation variable should be defined on a slide unless it is clear that everyone knows what it means. Jargon should be avoided. In my field we talk about thetas, etas, and omegas. These refer to the fixed effects, random effects, and variance components of a nonlinear mixed effect model. Speak these terms to anyone outside our field, even to statisticians who might be quite familiar with nonlinear mixed effect modeling, and you will get blank stares. Those terms mean nothing to them. Numbers and statistics should be presented in context whenever possible. For example, you report that the estimated rate of growth of some variable is 3% per year. What does that mean? Is that good or bad? Can it be put into context like 'The rate of growth is estimated to be 3% per year. compared to last year's rate of growth of 0.2% per year?' Lastly, estimates should be reported with their errors. Continuing the example, 'The mean rate of growth is estimated to be 3% per year with a rate of growth of at least 1% per year with 95% confidence.'

Slides should also be clear in the sense that people can read your slides from wherever they are in the room. This means choosing a font and a font size that everyone can read. Anecdotal evidence suggests that Calibri, which is the default font in PowerPoint, and Arial are easy to read fonts. How big your font size should be depends on the distance of the farthest person in the room and screen size. Dave Paradi has a series of tables on his website called www.pptfontsizetable.com that may help you choose the appropriate font size given the screen width and distance from the screen. As a simpler rule, Nancy Duarte in her book *Slide:ology* (2008) suggests that you put your slides in Slide Sorter View in PowerPoint and reduce the size to 66%. If you can still read the slides, then so can your audience. She also suggests that if you are regularly going smaller than 28-point font and using third-level bullets then you are not making a slide; you are making a document.

Concise. Keep your presentation concise. Think about how much time you have for your presentation and think about what you want the audience to remember. What can you realistically accomplish in the time frame given to speak, taking into account questions that might be asked? One rule of thumb is to have no more slides than minutes you are presenting – the so called "one-minute" rule. More often than not, as people's attention spans decrease, the number of slides per minute seems to be increasing. I've seen presentations with 150 slides in an hour. As you review your slides, ask yourself "Is this information needed for me to reach my main point?" If not, delete it. Think about how much time will be needed for each slide. More complex slides will need more explanation and therefore longer time. Do not allow yourself to go over your time limit as this will be disrespectful to the audience and to the next speaker. Don't be one of those guys that tries to do an hour's worth of slides in 30 minutes.

The "What Do You Do?" Challenge?

If you want some practice on making a statement clear and concise try the "What do you do?" challenge. In this challenge, imagine you meet someone new, who is not in your field, and they ask you "What do you do for a living?" How would you respond? Don't be glib and answer "I'm a scientist."

Think about how you would describe your job in just a sentence or two in a manner that really captures the essence of your work. Mine might be: "I work for a drug company. I use math to understand how a drug's dose relates to its effect and I use that to find the best dose for a patient."

Cultured. Cultured slides are slides that are sophisticated. You don't want to use fonts that aren't taken seriously like **comic sans font** or are too formal like any GOTHIC-STYLE FONT. Stick to fonts that are traditional and easy to read. While I like to use serif fonts like Times New Roman for my report documents (and books, including this one), san serif fonts like

Arial, **Tahoma,** or century gothic, appear easier to read in presentations because they are bigger and bolder than sans serif and the characters in a word don't run into each other and appear continuous.

Nancy Duarte, in her book, says that you should think like a designer when you make your slides. Your slides don't have to be a work of art or a thing of beauty, but they also shouldn't be garish and loud using colors that don't complement each other or have too many different colors. The colors you choose set the tone for your presentation. Fun colors, like orange or yellow, or down to earth colors, like green or brown, say something about your presentation. If you are giving a presentation to the company president you wouldn't want to give your presentation in your competitor's colors. Try to find colors that will appeal to your audience. If you don't know what those are, at least use colors that are harmonious together. Text colors should contrast sharply from the background, but you would never want to make a slide using red and blue combinations since this strains the eyes or red and green combinations since this also strains the eyes and some people with color blindness might not be able to distinguish the colors. PowerPoint does have color templates that have been chosen to work well together, so if you are not an artist at least use the themes provided to you.

Now that I've convinced you that you should use color sparingly and in a sophisticated manner, there is an exception. That is when you want to really emphasize something, but even then you have to be cautious. I learned this a few years ago when I was giving a talk on Effective Communication at the American Conference on Pharmacometrics in Tucson in 2008. I made my slides at home but didn't look at them again until I was on stage. In the middle of my slide deck, when I meant to present a flow chart on informative presentations, was Figure 19. This was not the slide I prepared. The slide I prepared had a similar color theme for all arrows and for all boxes, but this had every crazy color you could think of. I paused while my brain tried to process what was going on.

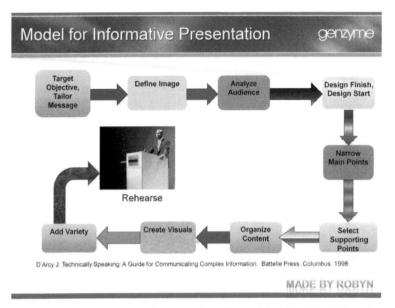

Figure 19. Slide made to illustrate the effect of loud and garish colors (and how sometimes they can be used to create a memorable image).

Then I noticed my 7 year old daughter's signature in the bottom right corner of the slide and I knew what had happened. At home, my daughter was just learning how to use PowerPoint on my computer. She would play with it all the time when I wasn't home. She loved to see the boxes and arrows fly across the screen. What must have happened was that my daughter had seen this slide on my computer while I was away from it and thought it needed more color, so she changed all the colors for me. When I figured out what had happened, I laughed and explained myself to the audience. Afterwards, and for months later, people would come up to me and talk about that slide. They remembered it because it was so dramatic. But what would happen if every slide was like this? That's right. The brain would overload from visual stimulation and none of the individual slides would be dramatic. When all the slides are dramatic then none are dramatic. When used sparingly a dramatic or bold color and/or pattern may be useful to create memorable slides.

Another thing you often see on slides is Clipart, those really simple hand drawings that are available in PowerPoint and are meant to embellish the main slide idea. The problem is they often add nothing other than making the slide look colorful. Edward Tufte refers to Clipart at 'Phluff' or slide clutter. I personally don't like Clipart. I think they look amateurish, but if I were going to use Clipart I would do so sparingly because since the drawings are so comical they tend to decrease the seriousness and credibility of your presentation. If you want your presentation to be informal, there is nothing wrong with using Clipart but don't overdo it since too many images can be distracting and try to have a consistent color theme for your Clipart images. If you want to add an image to embellish a main idea, consider a photograph instead. They are superior to Clipart in that there is a greater emotional connection to a picture than to a Clipart drawing. Finding a suitable image is not hard and a wide selection of public domain images can be discovered using Google Images. However, I would also avoid too many pictures on a slide because they can be overwhelming and potentially confusing.

Content. The last C is content which includes graphics, tables, and text. As the old quote goes "Content is King."[4] The content of your talk should be sufficient to reach your objectives. What follows is a discussion of many of the topics related to content, but I would be remiss if I didn't point out that the strategies in this book, for a more effective presentation, lie on the bedrock of excellent work. Without solid science then you are not selling your model, you're selling a lie.

A Few Words on Graphics

It was never my intent to write a book about how to make better and more effective graphics. To cover such material would require a book unto itself and indeed there are plenty of good books already written on that topic.

---

[4] This quote is often attributed to Bill Gates or Edward Tufte but has its origins much earlier (see the website http://www.craigbailey.net/content-is-king-by-bill-gates/, accessed 27 March 2014, for a discussion).

Books like Edward Tufte's (2001) *The Quantitative Display of Visual Information* or William S. Cleveland's (1994) *The Elements of Graphing Data* are classic texts on general principles of displaying data. Naomi Robbins (2005) book *Creating More Effective Graphs* is a great example of using Tufte's and Cleveland's principles with specific graphical examples. Krause and O'Connell (2013) is a good introduction to graphics in the life sciences, while Wong (2010) is a good introduction to the business field. The reader is advised to examine these books and to take Edward Tufte's workshop on *Presenting Data* if you can. Tufte's class was an epiphany and changed the way I viewed the presentation of scientific data.

I would be remiss if I didn't at least review the high-level guidelines from these references on creating and using graphics in modeling and simulation presentations. Here are some guidelines based on their recommendations:

- Make the data be king. This may seem obvious but you'd be surprised how often this maxim is violated. Don't censor the data. Don't let chartjunk obscure the data. And keep the data to ink ratio high, i.e., remove as much of the graph that doesn't result in loss of data information.

- Be truthful. Again this should be obvious, but it is too easy to make misleading graphs. I don't think many scientists would choose to do so on purpose. I think they just don't know any better. Examples of misleading graphs and just plain bad graphs can be found at Karl Broman's website at the University of Wisconsin (http://www.biostat.wisc. edu/~kbroman, accessed 30 September, 2014), Michael Friendly's Gallery of Data Visualization (http://www.datavis.ca/gallery/, accessed 30 September, 2014), and Robbins (2005).

- Avoid chartjunk. When you spend too much time pretty-ing your graphics, you are probably spending it on chartjunk and not maximizing data information. Example of chartjunk include 3D-bar charts, distracting patterns or shading in bar plots or histograms, unnecessary grids, unnecessary text, strange fonts, and ornamental shadings or backgrounds.

- Clarity of content. This is the flip-side of avoiding what Tufte (2001) refers to as chartjunk. Keep the graph simple and make the graph's point clear. For example, don't obscure data with labels. Don't obscure axis labels with data. Draw data to scale. Don't overuse color. Use colors that provide contrast and legibility. Make sure the color adds something to the plot. Don't use color just to make your graphics colorful. Also, don't forget that some people can't distinguish colors. There is a great website (www.vischeck.com, accessed 1 October, 2014) that shows how people with color-blindness view the world.

- Be consistent. Like your slides, your graphics should have a consistent theme. Symbols that relate to groups should not change from one graph to another. Use symbols that maximize their visual differentiation, e.g., use O for Group 1 and use ■ for Group 2.

- Label appropriately. The graph should have a caption that captures the message of the graph. All your axes should have consistent units and be labeled properly with those units. All groups should have appropriate legends and be labeled appropriately. If your data have error bars, note somewhere on the slide what the error bars represent, i.e., are they standard errors or standard deviations?

As you make your graphic, ask yourself "What do I want the audience to remember from this graph?" The answer to this question should help guide you in the development of your graph.

Don't Make Your Presentation the Next Pixar Movie

I love animation. On The Simpsons. On South Park. And in presentations *when done appropriately*. With PowerPoint you can animate everything. Bullets can fly in from the left, from the right, they can magically appear, fade in, all kinds of things. Just because you can do something doesn't mean you should, however. Too much animation will cause someone to get visual vertigo, as Duarte (2008) calls it. If you are going to use animation think about whether or not it's appropriate. Does it add value to the presentation, or are you just trying to make your presentation look cool? Does the movement distract the audience or help in the interpretation of the slide? If the animation doesn't add value, don't use it.

There is one exception for when animation is useful and that is when you have a slide of bullets and you want to introduce each bullet one at a time. When you have a slide with lots of text, the audience will read the slide and not pay attention to you. By introducing each bullet one at a time you keep the audience focused on the point you want to make and not move ahead of the presentation. In this case you want to use a simple animation like dissolve in or appear. You don't want the bullets to fly in because that is too distracting. Be careful not to overuse it and have it turn into a gimmick.

Model Acceptance and Believability

When an audience is presented with a model they will form an opinion that lies somewhere between acceptance and rejection of the model. If they accept your model, you can skip to the next section. If not, read on. Some of the reasons people don't accept a model are that they don't understand it, they don't believe it because it's too simple or it's too complicated, they're uneasy around models, or maybe they're just recalcitrant. If someone doesn't accept a model, how do you get them to turn around and start believing in the model? How can you change their mind?

Borrowing on the Technology Acceptance Model (TAM), which was developed to explain how individuals come to accept a new technology, a model is accepted in stages. As an individual progresses through the stages they become more and more accepting of the technology. A modification of the TAM applied to mathematical modeling is presented in Figure 20. In the first stage, Awareness, a person becomes aware that a model exists.

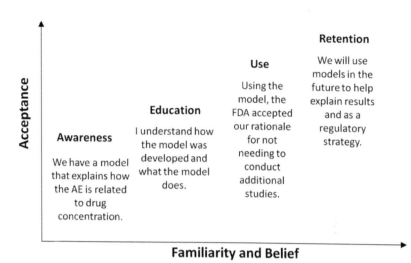

Figure 20. Paradigm for model acceptance. People first become aware of a model. They then start to understand how the model works, what are its limitations, etc. Then they start to use the model and recognize the value of the model. Finally, they take what they have learned about the model and want to use it and apply it to other situations.

They may first become aware of the model during a presentation made by a modeler, or by reading some report, or they may know that the modeler is going to develop a model for some system in the future. At the Education stage, they learn more about the model: how it was developed, how it was evaluated, what its characteristics are, what are its benefits, and what are its limitations.

At this point they progress to Figure 21 where they reflect on how complex the model is and whether or not the model assumptions and limitations are too great for acceptance. They evaluate the benefits of the model against its risks. They may evaluate whether the model conforms to their beliefs on how the model should be structured. If the model agrees with their beliefs they may show confirmation bias and accept the model. If the results of the model disagree with their previous beliefs they may exhibit cognitive dissonance (where there is mental discomfort when two or more beliefs are

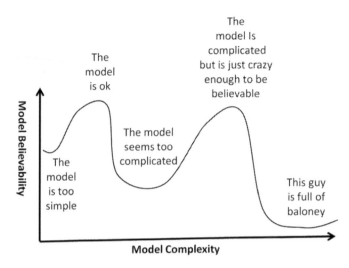

Figure 21. Paradigm for how model complexity affects model acceptance.

in conflict with each other) and look for flaws in the model rather than re-examine whether their beliefs are wrong.

As they become educated, hopefully their acceptance of the model increases. Next comes the Use stage where the person knows a model exists, understands the model, and uses the model. Generally this is where the TAM ends – with users using the model. However, with modeling there is one more step and that is the audience wants to use models in the future. There is retention of the model and its benefits. They are aware of the advantages that modeling can offer and are willing to use models in the future. Once a new model is developed or a different model for a different project altogether is developed, people start back at the Awareness stage but may progress more rapidly through the stages as they become more and more familiar with the model.

As was just mentioned, at the Education stage people evaluate the model for its complexity, which is an individual perception. How complex a model is varies from individual to individual. For an experienced modeler, a model may not be that complicated but to a non-modeler the model may

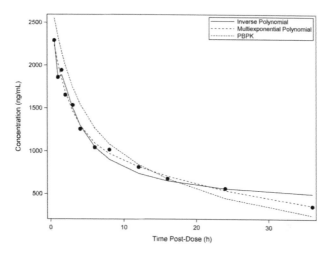

Figure 22. Experimental results for measurement of Drug X over time. Solid circles are the mean. Predictions are shown for an inverse cubic polynomial, polyexponential, and PBPK model.

be extremely complicated. Every person starts off at a different point on Figure 21. For the same model, some may be at the 'model is okay' stage while others may be at the 'model is too complicated' stage.

To illustrate the paradigm for model complexity, let's consider the data in Figure 22. In this experiment, a drug is given to a human subject and plasma concentrations of the drug are measured over time. Our goal is to develop a model that explains the concentration (C)-time (t) profile. This experiment is a study in pharmacokinetics. A simple model to describe such a profile is an inverse cubic polynomial of the form

$$C = \beta_1 + \beta_2 \frac{1}{t} + \beta_3 \frac{1}{t^2} + \beta_4 \frac{1}{t^3} + \varepsilon \tag{1}$$

under standard regression assumptions. When Eq. (1) is fit to the data, the resulting fit appears adequate. However, to a pharmacologist, they know that drug concentrations decay to zero over time. When this model is extrapolated beyond the time interval studied, it does not decay to zero but

95

asymptotes at β_1. Further, at t=0 the concentration is undefined when it should be zero. Hence, this model is too simple and too empirical.

For decades pharmacologists have reported that drug concentration-time profiles can be described by the sum of a polyexponential equation

$$C = \sum_{i=i}^{p} A_p \exp(-\alpha_i t) + \varepsilon .$$ (2)

where p is the number of distinct phases in the profile, 2 in this case. These equations have the necessary decay characteristics of a drug in the body and have a somewhat biological representation in that they are the mathematical expression of a compartmental system. When Eq. (2) is fitted to the data, it too is an adequate fit. There are hundreds of drugs whose concentration-time profiles are represented by such a model so there is a high degree of validity around such an equation. For many pharmacologists they would be satisfied with such a model and they are at 'the model is okay' stage.

However, Eq. (2) has no physiological meaning. It's a purely mathematical description of the data. Even if you take the equation to its compartmental representation, the compartments themselves have no anatomic or physiologic meaning. To some, however, even at this stage, the model may be too simple. In the 1960s and 1970s, a new class of pharmacokinetic models emerged, and compartmental models were expanded such that the compartments themselves took on anatomic meaning. Each compartment in the model represented some organ in the body. Each rate constant into and out of each compartment was a function of blood flow to that organ and the percent of cardiac output to that organ. Such models were called physiological-based pharmacokinetic models (PBPK) and a schematic of their structure is shown in Figure 23. In this PBPK model each compartment (represented as a square in the figure) and the mass balance to and from is expressed in the general form of a differential equation with

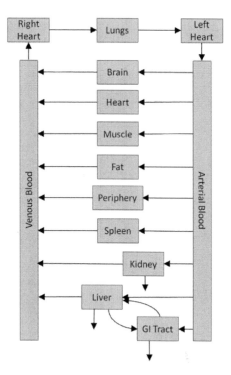

Figure 23. Example of a physiologically-based pharmacokinetic model.

the complete model having 14 such equations. When this PBPK model is fit to the data it too adequately predicts the data in Figure 22. To some, however, a PBPK model may be too complicated (why do you need 14 differential equations to describe just 12 data points?), but to some they may think "This model is complicated but is just crazy enough to be believable" stage. Whether they think the model is okay or too complicated is a matter of individual preferences. As an aside, it is worth discussing in Figure 21 the slope of the line around the two sweet points in the graph where believability is at a maximum and the "model is okay." The slope of the line to reach a sweet point is shallower than the slope of the line after a sweet point, when the model is on the path towards too much complexity. This is because it's easier to reject a model than to accept it.

One assumption of compartmental models is that once a substance enters the compartment it is homogenously distributed throughout the compartment. If each compartment is to represent a different organ in the body, then this assumption is violated. For example, it would not be expected that as a substrate passes through the liver the substrate concentration is homogenous throughout the entire liver. There would be a spatial gradient outwards from the liver canniculi. The PBPK model in Figure 23 could be expanded by representing what happens inside each compartment with a partial differential equation where substrate changes are modeled as a function of space and time. Such a model would be exceedingly complex and if someone were to present such a model, most experts in the area would think "this guy is full of crap." When someone reaches the "This guy is full of crap" stage they don't progress any further. They remain at that stage until they learn more about the model, are educated about it, and are comfortable enough to move back towards the acceptance point. They might learn that it is not so complicated after all. They might learn that such a complicated model is needed to solve a particular problem. They might begin to understand the model and its limitations and at that point move back to the "the model is okay but complicated" stage.

Although we would like to believe that when we make a decision, like the decision to accept a model, we do so objectively and without bias, the truth is that, when we look at new data and are internally arguing within ourselves about what decision to make there are a number of cognitive biases, decision-making short-cuts if you will, almost all of which we are unaware of, that point us in a particular direction. Daniel Kahneman, the second psychologist to win the Nobel Prize in Economics, spent his career detailing these biases and wrote about them in his book, *Thinking, Fast and Slow* (2011). These biases will be discussed later in this book in the section The Presenter's Paradox.

Like a car that pulls to the left as it drives down the road, cognitive biases act the same way in our decision-making process and. although there are dozens of different biases, we will focus on just two that impact model acceptance: confirmation bias and cognitive dissonance. The latter is when people favor results or information that fits in with their previously held beliefs. Confirmation bias is like an internal "yes man." If the structure of the model agrees with their predefined notions of what the model should look like or the results of the model agree with their beliefs, then a person is more apt to accept and use a model. This can play into your favor. So if you know someone has accepted a particular model or is familiar with a particular class of models, and this person is an important person needed for buy-in of the model, you may (if appropriate) wish to use the same class of models again with this person. Confirmation bias can also be carried over to people. Suppose a person has worked with a modeler and that modeler has been deemed credible and trust worthy. In the future they will be given the benefit of the doubt and are more likely trusted. Their models are more likely to be accepted. Of course, the flip-side is also true. If a person has worked with a modeler in the past and they trust that modeler, then if you are a new modeler taking over for the other modeler, if there is some negative situation it may be more difficult for you to right the situation in the other person's eyes. Confirmation bias can be overcome by being as objective as possible, by not presenting opinion as fact, and to sell yourself as credible and trust worthy.

Cognitive dissonance is that uneasiness you feel when two or more of your beliefs are in conflict with each other. Cognitive dissonance could arise when the structure of the model or the model results disagree with your previous held beliefs. When two such beliefs are in conflict we tend to find ways to minimize the conflict either through confirmation bias or rationalization. The classic example of cognitive dissonance is the case for smokers. Everyone knows smoking is bad for you but smokers tell you things like smoking calms me down, or I enjoy smoking, as a way to rationalize their behavior. They know smoking is bad for them but they choose to do it anyways for the perceived benefits of it. They may also minimize cognitive dissonance through confirmation bias, where they look for information that confirms their beliefs. They may cherry-pick

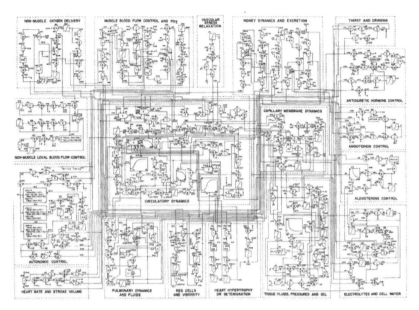

Figure 24. Alexander Guyton's model of the human cardiovascular system. *Reprinted with permission from the American Journal of Physiology, volume 34, copyright 1972 by Annual Reviews www.annualreview.com.*

information about smoking that causes them to feel that maybe smoking isn't so bad after all.

Let me give you an example. In the 1960s Alexander Guyton proposed a comprehensive model of cardiovascular function (Figure 24) that hypothesized a predominant role of urinary sodium excretion in blood pressure regulation, which up to that time seemed heretical, but later turned out to be right. Hearing such an effect in the model produced cognitive dissonance in physiologists as the hypothesis clashed with their prior beliefs. It's been said that models are particularly helpful when they generate new testable hypotheses. My own experiences suggest that such "new hypotheses" are useful if you are willing to accept the model as truth. This is the difference between physics and biologists. Physicists view the model, if correct, as truth and experimental data as a reflection of the model. Biologists view the data as the truth and the model as reflecting the data. In my experience when models and intuition clash, such discrepancies are often met with derision and that the model "is wrong." People are far more willing to accept that the discrepancy is due to model misspecification than to some new exciting scientific discovery by the model.

Guyton's cardiovascular model is kind of an extreme example of model complexity. When he presented his model he was ridiculed by the scientific community. His obituary states that "When he presented his mathematical model of cardiovascular function ... in 1968 ... responses ... reflected a tone of disbelief and sarcasm." That's probably putting it mildly. Even today, a model like that is difficult for most to believe. What may not be appreciated, however, is that a model doesn't have to be complicated to be too cutting edge, either. Even a simple model can be too cutting edge.

Let me give you another example. Early in my career my company was developing a new drug to treat schizophrenia. Many of the drugs used to treat schizophrenia prolong repolarization of the heart, which may lead to cardiac arrhythmia and sudden death. I was asked to analyze electrocardiogram (ECG) data from a clinical study of a new drug that was given to healthy volunteers at four dose levels: 0, 10, 30, and 60 mg. Throughout the study ECGs were collected on each subject in the study and analyzed by a cardiologist. We were interested in whether the new drug we were developing significantly prolonged cardiac repolarization and could potentially produce fatal arrhythmias.

An easily measured marker for cardiac prolongation is the QT interval on an ECG. If the QT interval is increased compared to baseline this is evidence that the heart is taking longer to repolarize. The problem is that QT intervals are affected by heart rate and they are highly variable both within- and between-subjects. As heart rate increases, the QT interval shortens, and vice-versa. To control for heart rate, QT intervals are standardized to some function of the RR interval (which is the inverse of heart rate). At the time the most common correction was Bazett's correction, which had been in use since 1927. Corrected QT intervals that adequately control for heart rate should have no correlation with RR intervals; when plotted against each other they should show a flat line. I noticed in my analysis that Bazett's correction was not working properly (see the top of Figure 25). That downward negative slope indicates the correction wasn't working in this study and that Bazett's QTc intervals were not being adequately controlled during the analysis. I also noticed that a lesser used correction formula called Fridericia's correction, which was developed the same year as Bazett's correction but used a cube root function on the RR interval instead of the square root function that Bazett's used with the RR interval, behaved better and actually corrected for RR intervals (bottom of Figure 25). It's been anecdotally said that in the 1920s when Bazett's and Fridericia's correction were published it was easier to calculate the square root of a number than the cube root and this is why Bazett's correction became the *de facto* standard. When corrected QT intervals with Fridericia's correction were plotted against RR intervals a flat line was observed, which is what you want.

At the time of my analysis, the head of research and development at my company was a cardiologist. When I presented my findings to him and the project team, I indicated that we should not use Bazett's correction and that we should use Fridericia's instead. I got an earful from the head of R&D, something to the effect of "I'll be damned if some kid out of school is going to tell me how to read an ECG." He wouldn't even consider my proposal. At that point all my credibility with the team was gone and I was told to analyze the data using Bazett's correction. The moral of the story is that even with a simple model, such as the correlation between two variables, a model may be too cutting edge. Modelers have to walk a fine line between developing a model that is too simple and one that is too complex. They need to find that sweet spot where the model is "just right." The problem is that one person's "just right" may be another person's too complex. I think modelers, especially young modelers, believe they get extra points when they develop complicated models so they tend to make things overly complex.

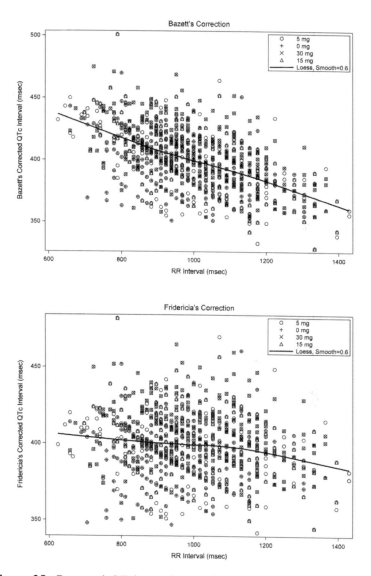

Figure 25. Corrected QT intervals as a function of RR intervals using Bazett's (top figure) and Fridericia's (bottom figure) correction. Each symbol represents a different dose group. Each data point represents repeated observations on multiple subjects.

103

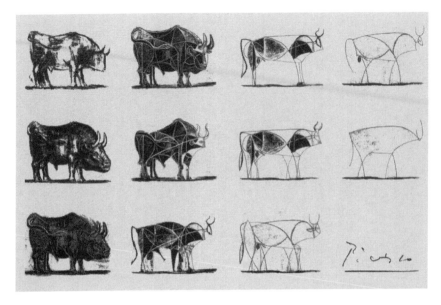

Figure 26. Pablo Picasso's deconstructed bull. Picasso shows us that you don't have to be complicated to get your point across. © *2012 Estate of Pablo Picasso / Artist Rights Society (ARS), New York.*

Figure 26 is Pablo Picasso's Deconstructed Bull. Picasso starts with a realistic bull and then removes elements making the bull simpler and simpler. Picasso shows us that you don't have to be complicated to be effective. He reminds us that extra points are given to those that have impact, not to those that are overly complex. He shows us that we don't always need the fully realistic bull to know that the drawing is of a bull. As the bull becomes more abstract, that the drawing is still of a bull is clear until there comes a point where it could be something else. Where that point differs is different for different people. Models are a lot like that. We can start out with an abstract model and progress to fully realistic models. At some point the properties of the model become apparent. Picasso also once said that "Art is a lie that makes us realize the truth." The same can be said of modeling. Most models are incomplete and do not truly represent reality. They are approximations that are designed to help us understand the truth of the system.

Suppose someone is stuck at the "model is too simple" or "model is too complicated" stage. What can be done to move them to the "model is okay" stage? One solution is to remove the objection(s) a person has to the model. This topic will be dealt with in more detail in a later chapter. Understanding the protests of the objector is helpful in understanding how the model can be improved. They might prefer that additional factors be taken into account in the model or that model terms be removed. Remember in so doing you may move another person from their sweet spot into a region where the model is too simple or too complex, or in the case where additional model terms are being added, the result may be an unstable overparameterized model.

Sometimes what is needed is not to change the model but to change the objector's way of thinking. If the model is too simple, there aren't many options available. The modeler may try to focus on the benefits of using a simpler model. For example, the simpler model may be easier to use, easier to program, and easier to manipulate than a more complex model. You could try to educate using Occam's razor – that models with fewer assumptions are preferred to more complex models. Unfortunately this argument rarely sways someone from their opinion because most people are obstinate in their opinions. Alternatively, you could propose to use both the simpler model and the more complex model and then compare the results from the two models. If the results of the two models are similar, you could propose that the simpler model will be used. If there are differences you could then try to understand the reason for the differences and see if the reason justifies the choice of the more complex model.

If the model is too complex then additional education must be provided to make the model less complex to the objector. You start by explaining the model. This may seem obvious, but being able to explain a difficult concept is hard and we take it for granted. We're not taught how to explain things in school and some people are simply better at it than others. You know that guy who, when asked to explain something that should take a few seconds, instead drags out the explanation and buries you with details? Scott Berkun (2011) calls these people 'complexifiers,' people who take something like x=y and turn it into (x+2)/(y+2)=1. Simplifiers, on the other hand, take complex ideas and simply communicate it without losing the main essence of the idea. I am firmly convinced that, as scientists, we are trained to be complexifiers. Why is that? One reason may be because we aren't trained to be simplifiers. In graduate school we are trained to focus on the details. Scientific writing by its nature is encouraged to be obtuse in the name of scientific rigor. Too bad that's just rubbish. Another reason may be because we want to appear smart. We want to show everyone, look at my model and see how smart I am. This attitude starts early in school with us wanting to impress our peers and the faculty and then continues well on into our careers.

We, as scientists, need to learn how to be simplifiers, which is not an impossible goal as there are great simplifiers in every field. Notable ones include Carl Sagan, Neil deGrasse Tyson, and Bill Nye the Science Guy. The late Carl Sagan was particularly brilliant in this regard. Here is how he described in lay terms the concept of cosmic time: "Imagine the 15-billion-year lifetime of the universe … compressed into the span of a single year. All recorded history occupies the last 10 seconds of December 31; and the time from the waning of the Middle Ages to the present occupies little more than one second." Today, Neil deGrasse Tyson has taken Sagan's mantle and is quoted all the time in the lay press to explain new astrophysics discoveries and their impact on science and society. I am not sure why the simplifiers in physics seem to get the most attention from the lay press, but surely there are some modelers who are great simplifiers.

How do you explain a model? Maybe I should first ask, have you ever asked someone for directions? Some people give you directions but you are still lost afterwards, while others give directions that make it perfectly clear how to get where you are going. Compare "Go North to 176, turn East to Route 45 and then North on Davis Street for a tenth of a mile. It's on the left." to "Keep going till you see the Dairy Queen, turn right, follow it two stoplights and turn left. That's Davis. Go about a block. It's the red building on the left." Which one is easier to understand? The second one is easier to understand because that person gave directions necessary from the point of view of the other person. The first person, who was familiar with the area, gave directions as if he himself was asking for directions. He was giving directions from his point of view, not the point of view of the driver asking for directions. Explaining a model is a lot like giving directions – you have to give them from the other person's point of view.

The problem with being able to explain a difficult thing is that we suffer from what Chip and Dan Heath in their book *Made to Stick* (2008) call the "Curse of Knowledge," which is simply that those who have the knowledge can't think about it from the point of view of those who don't have the knowledge. We forget what it was like to not know what we know. As a result, knowledgeable people often make mistakes assuming what other people know, usually assuming they know more than they do.

Does knowing about the curse, break it? I don't believe so. You have to do more than just know about the curse. You have to actively work to simplify and explain. Borrowing from Lee LeFever's book *The Art of Explanation* (2013), first consider the continuum of knowledge for a particular model:

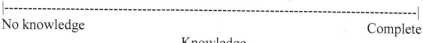

No knowledge   Complete

Knowledge

Suppose you are over there on the right by Complete Knowledge, you know everything about the model and are an expert modeler. On the far left are people who know nothing about models. They don't know what they are, how they are used, or how they are chosen. They know nothing. As a person moves from left to right the things they need to know to understand the model change. Being over there on the right, when we present a model we tend to focus on the "how." Here are the data I used to make the model. Here is the model development process. Here is the best model. Here is how I validated the model. Here are its predictions. As experts we tend to focus on details and features of the model. People on the left don't want to know about "how", they want to know "Why?" Without answering that first, the "how" will get completely ignored.

As an example, consider this presentation. Text in parentheses are meant for clarity and are not spoken by the presenter:

> "I modeled drug concentrations using a PBPK model with 14 organs (shows Figure 23) using SAAM II[5]. Here are the equations I used (shows a slide of 14 different differential equations) and here are the model parameters (shows a table of 32 parameters). All of the parameters were estimated with less than 50% CV and the bias after nonparametric bootstrapping was less than 5%. The condition number of my model was less than 1000. Using the model, I simulated the concentration in the brain (shows another figure of the concentration-time profile in the brain) assuming brain concentrations were twice that of plasma."

This explanation was short, simple, and to the point. If you knew the field, this might be a perfectly acceptable presentation. If you didn't know the field, was this helpful? Probably not. The audience would be asking themselves "What's a PBPK model? What's a CV? What is a condition number? Bootstrapping? What the hell is that? And how is nonparametric bootstrapping different than parametric bootstrapping? Ugh, so many equations – those are making my head hurt. And who is this Sam person? How did he help?" The modeler presented the features of the model and its results, but they also used a lot of jargon (never use jargon except if you are absolutely certain everyone will know what it means), and never went into "Why?" You hear descriptions like this all the time in my field. People who know nothing about modeling don't want to know "how," they first want to know "why." Why should I care? Why did you model the data? Why did you choose this model? Why? Why? Why? A good explanation first answers the question "Why?" It's only as people move towards the right do they want to start to know about "How."

---

[5] SAAM II is differential equation modeling and simulation software program (https://tegvirginia.com/solutions/saam-ii/).

Figure 27. An audience that is new to modeling doesn't want to know 'how,' they want to know 'why.' Why should I care? Why this model? Why do we even need a model? Why? Why? Why?

Now consider this presentation:

"Remember that we saw seizures in rats about 15 minutes after dosing at the highest dose level studied in the toxicology study? We need to know what the brain concentration was at the onset of seizures. Why do we need to know that? We need to know if there is any separation between brain concentrations that cause seizures and brain concentrations that inhibit our receptor target. If not we may not have a viable drug candidate and need to go back to the drawing board. Since brain concentrations weren't measured in any of our animal studies, we need to model the data we do have and then predict what the concentration was in the brain at the time of seizure. To model the data I used what's called a PBPK model, which stands for "physiologically-based pharmacokinetic model." If you don't know what a PBPK model is, it's really quite simple. All the major organs of interest in the rat are accounted for and then how the blood circulates into and out of each of then taken into accounted. Then we consider where metabolism and drug elimination occurs. Look, here's a picture (shows Figure 23). All total we have 14 different organs. The arrows are blood flow except for this arrow right here in the liver (pointing to an arrow in the figure) that leads to nowhere. That arrow accounts for metabolism of the drug and how the drug is eliminated from the rat.

A separate equation is needed for how drug moves into and out of each organ, so all total we have 14 equations. I won't show you the equations – that would just bore you and showing them is not needed to understand the model. What's great about a PBPK model is that it's mechanistic and accounts for the physiology and biochemistry of the rat. The down-side of a PBPK model is that it may be difficult to estimate all the variables in the model. There are 32 in this instance. To reduce the number of variables we have to model, we treated the blood flow into and out of each organ and the organ volumes themselves in the rat as a known constant. This reduced the number of estimable parameters to 14. I got the values of blood flow and volume in the rat from the Environmental Protection Agency's website because whenever the EPA studies a question like "What's the level of carcinogens in the lungs of second-hand smokers," they use a PBPK model and they need these constants for their models. So they've been compiling a list of these reference values for years and years.

Once we know how the drug moves into and out of each organ we can use simulation to estimate the drug concentrations in each organ over time and then using the dose of drug that caused seizures we can estimate what the brain concentration was 15 minutes after dosing. One of the key assumptions I made was that brain and plasma concentrations were in equilibrium and that brain concentrations were twice that of plasma. Why twice that of plasma? We did some cell culture work and found that concentrations inside man-made brain cells were twice that of outside the cell so it seemed reasonable to assume that brain concentrations would be twice that of plasma. Getting back to our problem, I was able to estimate the unknown parameters with less than 50% error and 5% bias. If my parameters had more than 50% error then that parameter essentially can't be estimated with any degree of confidence. In this case, all my parameters estimates had good precision and were without bias."

Notice the difference in these explanations. First they started off with "Why." Why did we need to model the data? Because we never measured brain concentrations in any of our previous studies and we have to predict it. Why did we choose this model and not some other model? Because the other models don't let us estimate brain concentrations and this model is physiologically realistic. Why don't we always use PBPK models? Because they have a lot of variables in them. Were all the variables properly accounted for? Yes, standard reference values were used. In the explanation, as we moved through the why's, we included some how's in there as well. How were the number of estimable parameters reduced? By fixing blood flow and organ values to physiological and anatomic constants. How were drug concentrations in the brain estimated? By assuming that brain concentrations were twice that of plasma. In this manner, the modeler provided background with details making the presentation easier to understand.

You may be asking yourself, how does this work when I have an audience with different levels of experience? The people with a high level of knowledge aren't going to want to hear all this introductory stuff. You may be right. Consider this situation. You have a group where some people have a high degree of modeling knowledge and others have a low degree. If you talk at the level of the high degree people, you will alienate the others and lose them during your presentation. If you take a few minutes to provide some background and talk about the basics to the people with a low degree of knowledge then you can have everyone in the room follow along. There is no negative effect in doing so and you don't risk losing anybody. There is the added benefit in that as you cover the background, to those who already know the material they will follow along and say to themselves "yes, I know this." It makes them feel good about the things they already know. It only takes a few seconds to say something like "I know some of you know a lot about modeling, but there are people in the room who do not. So please bear with me a few minutes while I give them some background on what we are trying to do." With that, you will put at ease the people with a high degree of knowledge and maybe even win some respect with them because you are showing respect for the others in the room.

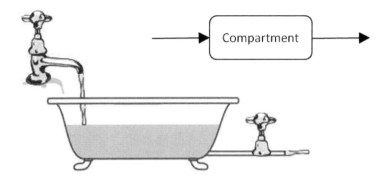

Figure 28. Compartmental models are often explained to lay people using a bathtub analogy. *Image reprinted from Linda Booth-Sweeney: Systems Thinking: A Means to Understand Our Complex World, Pegasus Communications, 2001.*

The key to explaining a model is to consider the model from the audience's point of view. Try to think back to when you were learning a particular model or class of models and what it took for you to understand it. Maybe you need to go back even farther to be able to explain it. How would you explain what a differential equation is if someone asked you? Would you say that it's based on the derivative or would you say something like it's the relationship between quantities and how those quantities change with respect to each other. The first explanation is rooted in the curse of knowledge, while, hopefully, the second explanation has the right amount of simplicity to be understandable.

One trick to explaining something to someone is to think in terms of analogies. Analogies demonstrate that two different things are quite similar for the purpose of clarification. Remember Carl Sagan's description of cosmic time? That was an analogy. Is the model analogous to anything else? If so, use the analogy to simplify the concept. For example, compartmental models are often described in terms of a bathtub where water is running into and out of the tub simultaneously (Figure 28). To use an analogy effectively, state the main analogy up front in one clear sentence and then expand to clarify the concept. Going back to the compartmental model analogy, you could say: "You can think of a compartment as a bathtub in which water is flowing in from the spigot and out through the drain at the same time. If the rate of water going into the tub is faster than the rate of water leaving the tub, the water level will rise. If the rate of water leaving the tub is faster than the rate entering the tub, the water level will drop." Most are familiar with this concept from when they had taken a bath and it is easy to make that leap in understanding from a tub to a compartment.

Another example of an analogy is the slide shown in Figure 29. Dean Bottino, a biomathematical modeler, was modeling changes in tumor size in cancer patients after treatment with an experimental drug. He was trying to think of a way that the project team would understand what he was doing and why. Coming from New Orleans he came up with Figure 29. This figure shows the similarities between changes in tumor growth prediction over time and prediction of hurricane landfall. It also shows how the model can be used to make more informed decision. With the hurricane model you may want to evacuate from where you currently are. With the tumor model you may want to change your dose. When shown this figure the team "got it." By making using an analogy the team was able to relate a new, abstract concept to something familiar, thereby facilitating acceptance of the model.

Another way to simplify something for an audience is to use metaphors and relate quantities to values the audience understands. Metaphors are a figure of speech, like a word or a phrase, used to make a comparison. Health risk experts do this all the time. For example, suppose you are an epidemiologist modeling the effects of speed limits on traffic fatalities and a state was interested in raising the interstate speed limit from 65 mph to 70 mph. You estimate this change could lead to an additional 3,000 deaths in the next three years. That kind of number is kind of abstract. To put it into perspective you could relate this number to the number of lives lost when the Two World Trade Center Towers fell during the 9/11 attacks. Most people in the U.S. could relate to this analogy really bringing home your message.

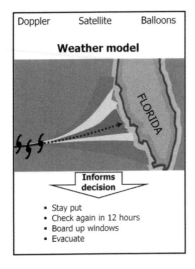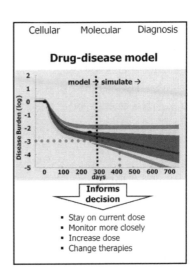

Figure 29. Figure used by Dean Bottino to explain the similarity between predicting tumor size over time in cancer patients after treatment with a new experimental cancer drug and weather models for hurricane landfall. *Image reprinted with permission of Dean Bottino.*

For really complicated models, however, analogies and metaphors are not going to be useful. You need to be able to explain the model visually. Most modelers when they present a complicated model do what I call the "everything at once" method (I used to call it the "vomit on the page" method but the "everything at once" method seems more professional, though not quite as colorful). No matter how complicated the model, they present the whole model to the audience at one time. It can be really overwhelming from the audience's point of view. Think of Guyton's cardiovascular model (Figure 24). It was pretty difficult to comprehend, wasn't it?

Dan Roam, in his best-selling book *The Back of the Napkin: Solving Problems and Selling Ideas with Pictures* (2009), says that complicated ideas are more easily explained if you draw them by hand using pictures as metaphors. He says that this method stimulates visual thinking by the participants and allows them to more easily comprehend difficult concepts.

I am going to partially agree with that statement. I don't think it's the drawing by hand that's important, I think it's that the complicated idea is built up piece-by-piece for the audience. I think Roam's idea of drawing by hand is so successful because it's novel. Who draws things by hand anymore? No one. Everything today is PowerPoint. For someone to stop and draw something by hand would cause you to put down what you are doing and pay attention. Who is this guy? Why is he drawing by hand? What's he drawing anyways? This idea is something old that's new again. It's interesting by its novelty and causes the audience to focus on what you are explaining.

Roam's idea of hand drawing a model could be used for a model like the stem cell differentiation model, shown earlier in the book in Figure 3 of the introductory chapter, but for larger models would be unwieldy. So here is where I start to differ with Roam's idea.[6] I think the use of hand drawing certainly helps in knowledge transfer but I think the real key to its success is that as you are drawing things what you are really doing is slowing down the explanation process, going through it step-by-step, allowing the audience to take the time to understand the concept. You could have a similar effect by breaking down a model into its components and, instead of throwing up the whole model at the audience at once, you can build the model to the audience up piece-by-piece in layers.

To illustrate the layering concept of building models I will use a cortisol secretion model as a tool to understand how a hypothetical drug might affect the hypothalamic-pituitary-adrenal (HPA) axis. It's not a difficult model but it nicely illustrates the layering process. I am going to demonstrate the layering process with a hypothetical presentation by a modeler who was part of a modeling development team and is now presenting their results to a project team. It's assumed that the standard

---

[6] It also depends on how well you can draw. If you're like me and everything you draw looks like a pig then the Roam method may be a hindrance.

jargon used by endocrinologists are known by the team but that not all the team members understand the specifics of the HPA axis.

First, a blank slide is shown to the team and the modeler begins speaking. "As you know we're interested in understanding how our drug affects the HPA axis. To answer this question we first developed a model of the HPA axis and then added onto that a pharmacokinetic-pharmacodynamic model of how our drug affects the HPA axis. So first I'm going to show you the HPA model. Let me start with the end of the system, cortisol, which measures adrenal function. In the blood, cortisol is released from the adrenals and is then metabolized and removed from the blood. This is shown here (the figure below is presented on the screen):

The oval here represents cortisol blood concentrations. The arrow into the oval is release of cortisol from the adrenal into the blood and the arrow out of the oval represents cortisol metabolism. If adrenal release is increased, blood cortisol increases. If adrenal release is decreased, cortisol concentrations decrease. Think of this like a bathtub. This arrow here (pointing to the arrow going into the compartment) is like the faucet and this arrow here (pointing to the arrow leaving the compartment) is like the drain. If we turn on the faucet in our bathtub, water will rise. Same thing here. If cortisol input increases, cortisol concentrations will increase. And if we open up the drain, water will drain from the rub. Same thing here. Increasing the output from the compartment will decrease cortisol concentrations.

Now moving up to the next level of the axis, at the level of the pituitary, ACTH is released from the pituitary into the blood and then metabolized. We modeled ACTH concentrations just like we did with cortisol - with an input and an output (next figure is shown):

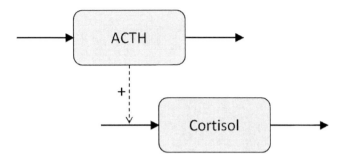

ACTH stimulates the release of cortisol from the adrenals, which is shown here with this dashed line. I use a dashed line, instead of a solid line, to show that this is an activation mechanism, and not a loss in ACTH concentration. Any changes in pituitary function should be reflected by changes in ACTH and cortisol concentrations. What questions do you have?"

Let me digress for a moment. Asking for questions from an audience is not as straightforward as it may seem. Notice I didn't ask "Are there any questions?" This is a simple yes/no question and people are less likely to respond. Instead I asked "What questions do you have?" This assumes people will have questions and subtly encourages the audience to ask them. Nevertheless, many people are uncomfortable being the first to speak or ask questions. You may want to try playing with the linguistics to encourage questions, such as "Do you have any thoughts on this so far?" Alternatively you might consider putting someone on the spot: "Mike, you look perplexed. Is there something I need to explain better?" Lastly, consider changing the dynamic entirely (Phillips, 2012). When you ask "Does anyone have any questions?" the audience wonders along with you, "Yeah, does anyone have any questions?" Instead, say something like "Now it's your turn. What should I clarify or go into greater detail on?" In this manner, the audience is given a direct command and the onus is on the audience to do something.

In responding to a question, and I probably don't need to say this but I will just to be clear, after the question is asked, don't do something stupid like roll your eyes or snicker at the question. Nothing will turn an audience off more than mocking or dismissing an audience member. Also, refrain from saying something like "That's a great question" or "that's a good question." It's natural to say something like this in an effort to connect with the audience and encourage more questions. It's condescending and if you don't say it every time, some people may think "why wasn't my question a good question?" It's best to simply avoid these after-question comments. If you want to "reward" the questioner, smile or nod in response.

Returning to the presentation, after answering any questions, the presenter continues. "Now, let me move up to the top most level of the axis – the level of the hypothalamus. CRH is released from the hypothalamus into the blood and metabolized. CRH concentrations were modeled just like how ACTH and cortisol were modeled - with an input and an output (next figure is shown):

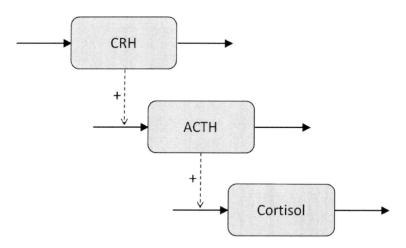

CRH stimulates ACTH secretion by the pituitary which I again show with this dashed line. We now have a three level model. However, the model isn't complete because there are some negative feedback loops to consider. Cortisol inhibits the release of CRH and ACTH. So if cortisol concentrations increase, CRH and ACTH release is decreased to compensate. This negative feedback loop (shows next figure) is shown here as a heavy dashed line and note that it has a negative effect by this negative sign. Thoughts or questions on what was done so far?" Then someone speaks up. "I do. How do you know the order is right? That CRH affects ACTH and that ACTH then affects cortisol? What happens if the order if wrong?" The speaker then replies: "This pathway is very well established by physiologists. It's been known for a really long time. Also, this particular mathematical formulation of the system is pretty well established too. Does that answer your question?" The questioner nods and then the speaker moves on to the slide shown below:

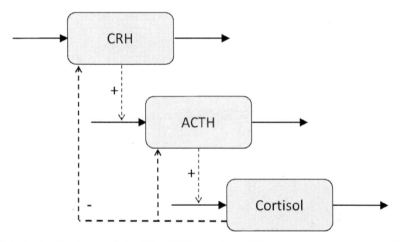

"This is the basic model of the HPA system. Now we move onto our drug and how it affects the system (Figure 30 is shown). Our drug is a CRH antagonist that blocks the release of cortisol. When we give our drug by infusion it's metabolized by the liver. So I modeled the pharmacokinetics of our drug like the kinetics of CRH, ACTH, and cortisol - with an infusion input and a metabolism output. I used a different color for the oval box to denote that this is our drug. I then blocked the effect of CRH release. And that is the basic model. What questions are there?"

This is the layering process of model development. It starts with one part of the model and then the model is built up for the audience one layer at a time until the whole model is presented. Imagine this presentation using

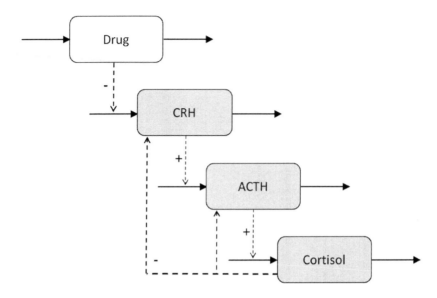

Figure 30. Final cortisol secretion model shown to the audience that is consistent with Gestalt principles. Notice the harmony in the figure and consistency across graph elements.

PowerPoint's Custom Animation feature where each figure can be overlaid on top of each other and made to appear at the click of a mouse. As the modeler discusses the model and new components are added, they appear on the screen on top of what has already been shown. It would look pretty nifty and it gives the audience time to digest what is being said. If there are questions, they can be answered before moving on. The audience has a chance to really understand the model.

Now consider the case where the modeler uses the "everything at once" approach and begins with "Here is my model. Let me show you how this works." Figure 30 is then shown on the screen in its entirety. The audience is thinking to themselves: "What are the black lines?" "What are the dashed lines?" "Are the plus signs positive activation and the negative signs negative feedback loops?" The audience would have so many questions. As you explain the model they are probably not even paying that

Figure 31. Gestalt Theory of Perception states that the individual parts have different perception when viewed as a whole. A tree is composed of branches, leaves, and roots, but when we see a tree we see "a tree," not "branches, roots, and leaves." We see the tree as a whole.

much attention to what you say as they try to make sense of the model by themselves and yet this is the approach many modelers use when presenting a conceptual model.

If you want to further improve understanding of a model, it helps if the model follows the Gestalt Theory of Visual Perception, which arose from psychologists in the 1920s and basically means that the parts have different characteristics from the whole. You probably have seen Gestalt figures but may not have known that's what they were. Think about a tree (Figure 31). Trees are made of branches, roots, leaves, maybe fruit or flowers. But when we see a tree, we don't see the branches, the roots, the leaves, we see a tree. We see the tree as a whole in its entirety. That's Gestalt – seeing things in the whole as something more than the sum of its parts. We see those secondary things but they're not as important as the whole.

Gestalt perception has six principles and they are all based on the theory of grouping:

1. **Proximity**: Things that are seen close together are seen as grouped together. For example: when we see

    1 2   3 4

    We see 1 and 2 as belonging to the same group and 3 and 4 belonging to the same group by virtue of their proximity.

2. **Similarity**: Things that are similar, either by shape, scale, or color, look similar when seen together. For example, when we see:

    ●○●○●○●○

    Our brain perceives all the ● as being the same and all the ○ as being the same, despite all of them being circles.

3. **Common fate**: If proximity and similarity are present, then movement can take place. For example, when we see:

    The circles would appear to move down and form another group.

4. **Group continuation**: A few interruptions do not change the reading of the whole. For example, when we see

    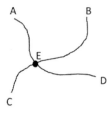

    Most people see the line segment AD as being one line and the line segment BC as being one line. Most people don't see line AE or line ED as two separate lines, despite the stoppage with ● at the end of line AE.

5. **Closure**: We tend to fill in discontinuous line segments. For example, when we see:

In the circle drawing, our brain tends to fill in the circle and we see it as a complete circle. In the bottom, we see two rectangles at angles to each other, not as 3 potential shapes touching each other.

6. **Figure/Ground and Area**: Figure and ground refer to positive elements and negative space. When first looking at an arrangement the eye separates whole figures from their background to make sense of the arrangement. Look at the figure below on the left:

 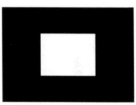

This arrangement is unstable. We either see the two people facing each other or we see the vase. We don't see both at the same time. Area refers to how the smaller of two overlapping objects is seen as the figure while the larger object is seen as the background, as illustrated in the figure above on the right. This figure is also stable. The more stable the relationship the easier for the brain to comprehend.

You're probably asking yourself, what does this have to do with modeling? The point is this, when drawing our conceptual models we should use Gestalt principles to make it easier for the audience to understand the model.

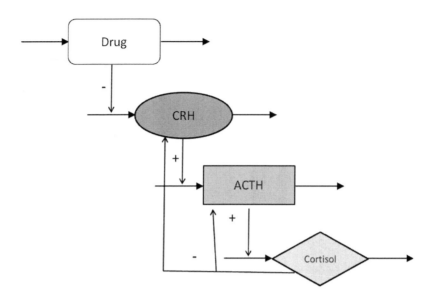

Figure 32. Cortisol secretion model drawn in a manner that violates Gestalt principles.

Figure 32 shows the same model as Figure 30 but one that is not consistent with Gestalt perception principles. They're the same model, but Figure 32 is more difficult to understand. The + signs are not close to the arrows (violation of proximity) so it's unclear to which arrow they belong to. The different shapes (violation of similarity) suggest that everything is different. All the lines are the same color and style (violation of sameness) suggesting that they all act the same way. The uneven lines are somewhat amateurish. If a few simple changes are made, the figure is much easier to understand (see Figure 30). We recognize where the + signs belong by virtue of their proximity to the arrows. We recognize that CRH, ACTH, and Cortisol are similar by them having the same shape and color. We recognize that the drug compartment is different because it has a different color and shape. We recognize that there is a difference between the dashed and solid arrows. In short, we might not comprehend the model, but on some level we are beginning to.

Moving now away from presenting conceptual models, what if the model is not a conceptual model but an equation? How do you explain an equation? It might not seem immediately obvious but some equations can be explained using metaphors. Suppose you had to explain a discrete Fourier series to someone. Fourier series are used in signal processing, earthquake analyses, and data compression. Suppose someone asked you "What is it and what's it good for?" How would you respond?

Mathematically, a discrete Fourier transform (DFT) can be written as:

$$X_k = \sum_{i=0}^{N-1} x_n \exp\left(-i2\pi kn / N\right). \tag{3}$$

How are you supposed to explain this crazy equation to someone? Wikipedia's definition:

> *"The DFT converts a finite list of equally spaced samples of a function into the list of coefficients of a finite combination of complex sinusoids, ordered by their frequencies, that has those same sample values."*

is not very useful, except to the most mathematically inclined. Kalid Azad, on his website, www.betterexplained.com, does an absolutely brilliant job by comparing a discrete Fourier transform to finding the ingredients of a smoothie, a fruit drink. As he explains, suppose you were drinking a smoothie and wanted to make one yourself. For that you would need to know the ingredients. Now suppose you have some filters lying around and that if you poured your smoothie into each filter the separate ingredients poured out (Figure 33). Once we know the ingredients we could make the smoothie ourselves.

Essentially that is what a discrete Fourier transform does – it breaks down a signal into a set of components that when added together make the original signal. It takes the signal from one point of view and transforms it to another point of view. This analogy is so simple and so informative.

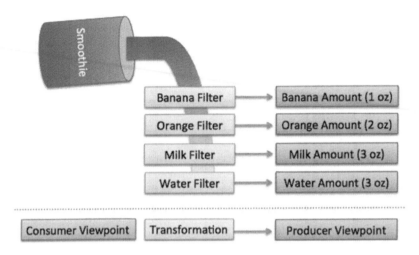

Figure 33. Figure used by Kalid Azad to explain how the discrete Fourier transform works. Imagine you wanted to know the ingredients of a smoothie and wanted to make one yourself. Suppose you had these filters lying around such that if you poured the smoothie into them, the separate ingredients would come out. Once you know the ingredients you could mix them together to make your own smoothie. This is what a discrete Fourier transform does. *Image reprinted with permission of Kalid Azad.*

You don't have to explain the equation – "The Fourier transform is the sum of a series involving exponents and complex numbers." By using the analogy, the transform is explain into something a kid could understand. Now granted this may not satisfy someone who was looking for a little more detail, but it gets you started. The audience now has a good feeling for what the transform does, even if they don't quite understand the math. Hopefully this will form the foundation so that later on they will get the big idea behind it.

Another good example of explaining equations was a monthly column called *Equation* that used to appear in Wired magazine (Conde Nast Publications, www.wired.com) from 2010 to 2011. It was a single magazine page that took an equation and explained it to the reader, simply, informatively, and in a fun manner. Figure 34 is an illustration from the

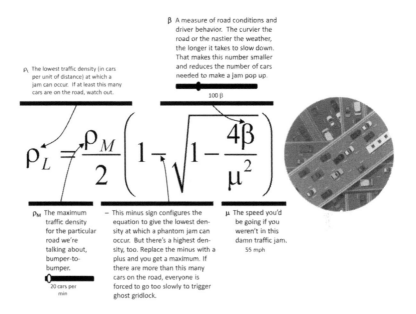

Figure 34. Illustration from Wired magazine. Developed by researchers at the University of Alberta and Massachusetts Institute of Technology the equation explains "phantom traffic jams." Their model explains how small disturbances like a driver hitting his brakes can ripple into a full-blown traffic jam. Notice in the graphic how variables are identified and explained. The cutesy drawing on the right side of the illustration shows a highway and cars on it illustrating that this equation relates to cars and traffic. *Illustration reprinted with permission from Julie Rehmeyer, Wired magazine, Conde Nast Publications, 22 June 2010© (http://www.wired.com/ magazine/2010/06/st_equation_traffic/, accessed 1 October, 2014).*

June 2010 issue showing Julie Rehmeyer's explanation of a Phantom Traffic Jam on a freeway, where traffic suddenly slows to a crawl and then was suddenly speeding again. The equation explaining Phantom Traffic Jams was developed by Morris Flynn at the University of Alberta and others (Flynn et al., 2009). Their website offers further details of the model if you are interested (http://math.mit.edu/projects/traffic, accessed 1 October, 2014).

Ten Ridiculously Simple Things You Can Do To Instantly Improve The Quality Of Your cPresentations

1. Move your main message to the start of the presentation
2. One message per slide whenever possible
3. No more "Walls of Numbers"
4. All graphs and tables have the message as the slide title with no more than a single message per slide (Figure 35a and b)[7]
5. All slides readable from the back of the room
6. Don't go over your time limit
7. Have consistent font, styles, and colors
8. Ask yourself, "Do I really need this slide?"
9. Don't let the message get lost in the medium
10. Remember 'simplicity'

Other columns from past issues were on how rainbows are made, how to calculate a skyscraper's sway, and how the Federal Aviation Administration estimates the number of casualties from getting hit by space-junk coming back to Earth. What was fantastic about these columns was that they took some phenomenon (like how rainbows are made), showed that it could be explained by some model (Snell's Law), and then broke down the model into its components into a graphical form that was easily digestible to the reader.

The layering technique can also be applied to equations. Each piece of the formula can be introduced one-by-one, so as to not overwhelm the audience. You can also include a bit of story-telling to engage the audience. For instance, going back to the Phantom Traffic problem, you could say "The other day I was driving down the freeway and all of a sudden traffic stopped. I thought there was an accident ahead. Then, all of a sudden, we started moving again. I looked for an accident, but there was

---

[7] This rule is sometimes referred to as the McKinsey Rule, a reference to graphs produced by the management consultant company, McKinsey & Company.

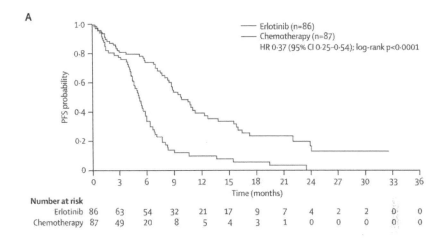

Figure 35a. Every graph and table should have a slide title containing the main message. Plot A is a Kaplan-Meier plot of progression-free survival (PFS) following erlotinib treatment compared to standard chemotherapy in patients with non-small cell lung cancer (Rossell et al., 2012). Many scientists would use a slide title like 'Kaplan-Meier Plot of PFS.' While that is indeed what this is a figure of, it doesn't tell the message. A slide title like 'Erlotinib prolongs PFS by 4.5 months' is much more forceful and really sends home the message. *Reprinted with permission; Elsevier copyright 2012.*

none. We just all inexplicably came to a stop and started moving again. This was a phantom traffic jam. Researchers at the University of Alberta and MIT have developed a formula to explain such phantom traffic jams based on fluid flow dynamics and how at high flow rates small perturbations in the flow have a ripple effect. They call them traffic roll waves." Or you can turn the idea around and pose the question to the audience like "Who here has been driving down the freeway and all of sudden traffic stops and then inexplicably starts again? Anyone? Of course, we've all been in that situation. Researchers at the University of Alberta and MIT have developed a formula to explain such phantom traffic jams." After breaking the ice, you can then move into the meat of your presentation and present the equation and how it was formulated, its assumptions, etc.

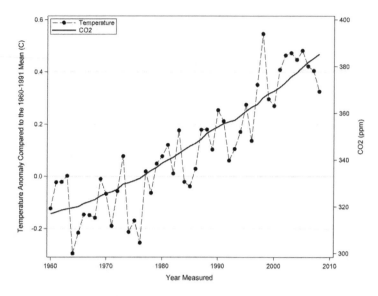

Figure 35b. Every graph and table should have a slide title containing the main message. In the plot above, someone might provide a slide title like "Time-Series of Temperature and Atmospheric CO_2 Since 1960." But there are many messages that could be drawn from this graph: CO_2 concentration and temperature are positively correlated, temperature and CO_2 have generally risen since 1960, and temperature and CO_2 have generally risen since 1960 but temperature has dropped while CO_2 continues to rise after 2005. Each of these conclusions has important implications and different people will draw different conclusions. Putting the message as the slide title forces the viewer to know your meaning. *Data from (BBC News, 12-3-2009).*

Lastly, instead of trying to explain the model better, another way to move a person to a sweet spot is to explain the benefits of the model. Salespeople talk about the features and benefits of a product (Vass, 1998). The features are about the product: its physical attributes, technical details, etc. The benefits are what the buyer cares about. What will it do for the buyer? For example, Theodore Levitt, a Marketing professor at Harvard, once quipped "people don't want to buy a drill. They want a quarter-inch hole." This brilliant quote summarizes the point of view from the buyer. Too often when we are trying to sell someone something we focus on the features of the product, when the buyer wants to know "what's in it for me?"

When applied to modeling and you are trying to move someone from a spot of resistance to a spot of acceptance, especially if they are a layperson, don't focus on the details. Focus on the benefits. With this model we can predict sales for the next year. With this model we can say with 80% certainty that a dose of 100 mg will be effective in at least 80% of the population. With this model we can predict that this river is going to overflow its banks in the next month given the current precipitation record. The benefits are what the buyer cares about, so it may be easier to sell a person on the benefits, instead of trying to get them to understand the technical features of the model.

Einstein once said that "if you can't explain it to a six year old, you don't understand it." It's pithy and is often repeated. But it's wrong. Think about it. 75 years ago, Einstein had to explain $E=mc^2$. Today we have fields like systems biology, nonlinear mixed effects modeling, chaos theory, just to name a few. This is difficult stuff to explain and no amount of simplification will allow a six year old to understand it. Nevertheless, his point is well taken. We should be able to explain our models to others in a way they understand. Whether we build the model up in layers or use analogies or metaphors, or whatever we need to do to make a model understandable, we should be able to explain a model to an audience without boring them to death or losing them along the way such that they don't ever care to be found. Remember to start from the point of view of the audience and ask yourself "Why?" and then move into the "How."

The Presenter's Paradox

Answer the following question:

> *A bat and a ball cost a $1.10.*
> *The bat costs $1.00 more than the ball.*
> *How much does the ball cost?*

Quick. What's your answer? If you're like most people, you said a dime. 10¢. That's wrong. The correct answer is 5¢, a nickel. The first time I heard this problem, I said a dime as well. And when I was told the answer was a nickel, I said 'No way. It's a dime.' It was only when I sat down and did the math that I realized I was wrong and it was indeed a nickel. Consider this problem:

> Linda is 31 years old, single, outspoken and very bright. She majored in philosophy. As a student she was deeply concerned with issues of discrimination and social justice, and also participated in anti-nuclear demonstrations. Which scenario is more likely: (1) Linda is a bank teller, or (2) Linda is a bank teller and a feminist.

Quick. What's your answer? No cheating. Most people answer #2, Linda is a bank teller and a feminist. This too is wrong. Basic probability states that the probability of two events is less than or equal to either of the events alone. In other words, the probability of being a bank teller and a feminist has to be less than or equal to the probability of being a bank teller alone.

Don't feel too bad if you got these two problems wrong. More than 50% of students at Harvard, MIT, and Princeton failed the "Bat and Ball Problem." A total of 85% of students in Stanford's Graduate School of Business failed the "Linda problem." So if you got it wrong, you're in good company. The question is, why did you get them wrong?

Daniel Kahneman a psychologist at Princeton University, and Amos Tversky, a psychologist at Hebrew University and later Stanford University, started in the 1970s to study why people make the decisions they make and the cognitive biases that influence such decisions. Their research eventually led to Kahneman being awarded the Nobel Prize in Economics in 2002. In 2011 he published his-best selling book *Thinking, Fast and Slow*, in which he recounts his research.

Kahneman and Tversky proposed that humans largely think intuitively and that intuition is imperfect. They proposed that there are two systems for how our brain thinks, which they call System 1 and 2. The title of Kahneman's book is a reference to these systems. System 1 is fast, while System 2 is slow. System 1 is intuitive, works with little effort, is automatic, and works unconsciously. System 2 in contrast is "lazy," deliberate, takes effort to get into action, and is slow and controlled. These two systems do not correspond to some specific anatomic part of our brain but are like computer operating systems that share the same hardware (neural connections). Although these systems will be presented as distinct entities, they in fact work both in parallel and in conjunction with each other, and tasks can be shuffled between them.

The "Bat and Ball problem" and the "Linda problem" are questions devised by Shane Fredrick at Yale University and are part of the Cognitive Reflective Test, a type of intelligence test that challenges System 1 and System 2 thinking. Most people fail these problems and answer incorrectly because they fail to activate System 2 thinking. They are just simple enough that people intuitively think they know the answer without deeper thinking. Some people criticize the test because the questions are "trick questions." That is indeed the point, but an even simpler example of System 1 and System 2 thinking is the following. Look at the picture below:[8]

Quick. What do you see?

You can tell almost instantly that this is a picture of a child and that the child is sad. Now consider the following math problem and solve it in the next few seconds:

$16 \times 18 = ?$

What is your answer? Quickly.

---

[8] Image reprinted from Holly Chaffin, www.publicdomainimages.net.

Figure 36. I wonder if Kahneman and Tversky were Trekkies? Kirk and Spock in Gene Roddenberry's TV Series Star Trek are the embodiments of System 1 and System 2. Kirk (William Shatner, on the right) is intuitive, acts emotionally, he is quick to rush to judgment, and has an answer for everything. When he doesn't have an answer, like to the Kobayashi Maru problem (if you know what this is you pass the Geek of the Week test), he cheats. Spock (played by Leonard Nimoy, on the left) is controlled, precise, thoughtful, and above all, logical. *Image reprinted from Wikimedia Commons.*

The answer was 288. Did the answer just spring to mind? Probably not. These two problems nicely illustrate the difference between System 1 and System 2 thinking. The photo activates System 1; our answer is instantaneous, effortless. The math problem activates System 2; it takes time and effort to solve.

Most decisions in life are made using System 1, whereas System 2 works less often and only when circumstances require it. System 1 tries to solve every problem it encounters, whether right or wrong. What does the following phrase say?

THE BRAIN IS A MACHINE FOR
~~IUMRING TO GONCIUSIONS~~

Did you think it said that "System 1 is a machine for jumping to conclusions?" If I remove the black bar covering the bottom line, this is what it actually says:

THE BRAIN IS A MACHINE FOR
IUMRING TQ GONGIUSIQNS

Because of the context, you did indeed jump to a conclusion. Did you even consider for a second that maybe the letters were nonsensical? No, because System 1 likes causation since causation leads to cohesion. A sensical first line and nonsensical second line makes no sense to System 1. Saying that "System 1 is a machine for jumping to conclusions" goes together and that stops System 2 from activating.

System 1 answers whether or not it has all the information it needs to solve a problem. Consider this scenario: "Joey had an argument with his brother. The next day he came to school covered in bruises." As you read these sentences you probably assigned causation - Joey had bruises because his brother hit him. I didn't say that. I didn't say that the bruises were caused by his brother. The argument could have just been verbal. Joey could have gone to hockey practice later in the day, after the argument, and gotten the bruises there. Why did you assign causation? Because that's System 1 in action. System 1 assigns causation. System 1 likes a nice, neat coherent story. Our brain doesn't like it when things don't make sense. Then it has to activate System 2 and our brain doesn't like to activate System 2 because that takes more effort and energy. If I had said "Joey was playing ping-pong. The next day he came to school covered in bruises." you would have said "What? Wait a minute. Why was he covered in bruises?" and you would have questioned the causality. This incoherence was enough for you to activate System 2.

Why does our brain do this? If System 2 is the reasoning part of our brain and System 1 is the emotional, intuitive part of our brain, why don't our brains use System 2 more often? Why aren't we more rational thinkers? It probably has to do with evolution. Our brains needed a way to quickly size up and assess a situation without a lot of mental effort. System 1 can perform many different tasks quickly like tell us if someone is an obvious threat, do quick calculations, orient us to sudden sounds, respond to fill-in the blank phrasing, or recognize objects, just to name a few. And most of the time System 1 gives us pretty good results. Also, System 2 takes a lot of energy to activate and keep running. It would be exhausting to constantly have System 2 running to keep System 1 in check. So our brains keep System 1 in a constant state of activation and System 2 in a low activity state to be activated when needed.

System 1 has rapid access to a huge bank of memories it bases its judgments on and memories associated with strong emotions are the easiest to access. Kahneman gives the following example in his book. Think of these two words:

Bananas   Vomit

Almost without thinking, you probably associated bananas with vomiting and assigned a temporal, causal association to the words in that eating bananas caused vomiting. You may have visualized a banana. You may have actually have gotten a little bit nauseous thinking about vomiting. Your sympathetic nervous system may have become activated and your heart may have started to race a little. You may have remembered a time when you drank too much or had food poisoning and were vomiting. For a time being, in the future, you may continue to associate vomiting with bananas or with the color yellow or with other fruit associated with bananas like plantains. Try as you might, you cannot stop these associations. Ideas that are triggered in the brain evoke a cascade of other ideas, which in turn activate their own cascade of ideas, hence, giving rise to the term 'associative activation.' Think of how this system might react if you saw a picture of a growling tiger. It's pretty remarkable when you stop and think about it.

One thing about System 1 though is that every element in these associations is cognitively coherent. When our brain sees something that triggers System 1, it quickly searches through our memory bank for a memory coherent with the situation. Our memories then give rise to coherent emotions which are turned into coherent judgments. When we saw "Bananas Vomit," we didn't think "doorknob." That would have been incoherent. System 1 evokes a series of ideas and memories that are cognitively consistent. It's like having your own internal "yes man." System 1 ties up these ideas and memories into a neat tidy package.

It was only when you were surprised that System 2 became activated. Because you may have never associated bananas and vomiting before, at some point after the initial wave of ideas and memories, you became surprised and possibly thought an error was made. System 2 became activated and asked yourself "Wait, what? Bananas and vomiting. Did that really happen?" System 2 doubts everything. System 1 acts as a system of confirmation of beliefs. System 2 looks for disbelief. It's only when those involuntarily formed intuitions, feelings, and impressions are confirmed by System 2 that they are turned into attitudes and beliefs.

Because System 1 is based on impressions, intuitions, and memories it is susceptible to bias and errors in certain circumstances. For example, suppose I showed you the word
    EARTH
and then showed you this word with a missing letter
    S_N.
If I asked you what was the word with the missing letter you would be likely to have said 'SUN'. However, if I had first said
    MURDER
and then showed you
    S_N,
you would have been likely to say 'SIN'. By showing you these first words you were primed in your memory for the second word. This is an example of priming and System 1 is prone to priming errors.

Here's another example of how System 1 is prone to bias. Suppose I asked you what is the product of 8×7×6×5×4×3×2×1, what would your answer be? Stop. Really, what would your answer be? When Kahneman and Tversky asked this question to people, their average answer was 2,250. Now suppose I had asked you what was the product of 1×2×3×4×5×6×7×8, what would your answer be? When Kahneman and Tversky reversed the order of the multiplication and asked this question to students, their average answer was 512. The correct answer is 40,320. By starting with the number 8, most people were more likely to give a higher result than when starting the problem with the number 1. This is called an anchoring bias. By anchoring the first number, it serves as a reference point and changes the result. Surprisingly, the anchor doesn't even have to do with the problem. Tversky and Kahneman asked people to spin a ball on a roulette wheel with numbers from 1 to 100. They had secretly rigged the wheel so that the ball always landed on either the number 10 or the number 65. They then asked subjects how many nations in Africa were members of the United Nations. Subjects whose ball had landed on number 10 responded on average that 25% of African countries were in the United Nations, while subjects whose ball landed on 65 responded on average that 45% were members of the United Nations. Subjects whose ball landed on 65 had a significantly higher estimate than those whose ball landed on 10. Even this seemingly random event had the effect of anchoring their opinion.

It doesn't stop there. There are many such cognitive biases. In fact, Wikipedia lists more than 200 decision-making biases, social biases, and memory errors (http://en.wikipedia.org/wiki/List_of_cognitive_biases, accessed 30 September, 2014). It's a lot of fun to read about the different ones because with near certainty you have probably fallen victim to every one of them at some time or another. I would have to say after reading about all the different biases and errors, I was amazed that System 1 works as well as it does.

Another concept that Kahneman introduces in his book is cognitive ease and cognitive strain. Our brains are constantly examining the world around us. When a problem is introduced System 1 examines its level of difficulty to determine whether System 2 needs to be brought in for the hard thinking. Cognitive ease is when the problem is easy and can be solved by System 1. Cognitive strain is when the problem is hard and System 2 needs to be activated. When cognitive ease is present, we feel good, things are effortless, and they feel familiar and true. Factors that increase cognitive ease are primed ideas, clear display, familiarity, and a good mood.

Knowing about cognitive biases, and how they can trip up System 1, and the factors that increase cognitive ease is a good thing because we can use our knowledge to design our presentation to our advantage. For example, if a clear showing increases cognitive ease then an unclear showing will decrease cognitive ease, increase cognitive strain, and activate System 2. For example, remember the "Linda Problem" and the "Bat and Ball Problem" from Shane Frederick's Cognitive Reflection Test? There was one more problem to the test:

> In a lake is a patch of lily pads. Every day the patch doubles in size. If it takes 48 days for the patch to cover the entire lake, how long would it take for the patch to cover half the lake?

Most people think 24 days, but the answer is 47 days. When Frederick showed this problem to people, half in a clear font like above and half in a font that was hard to read:

> In a lake is a patch of lily pads. Every day the patch doubles in size. If it takes 48 days for the patch to cover the entire lake, how long would it take for the patch to cover half the lake?

Knowing what we know about cognitive strain, you might not be surprised to find out that 90% of those questioned got the problem wrong using the clearer more legible font, but only 35% did when they were shown the harder to read font. That's because with the harder to read font, cognitive strain was increased, System 1 quits trying, and System 2 becomes activated. People will think harder when presented with a hard to read font.

So should you use a hard to read font in your presentation? Maybe, but I wouldn't use it more than once in a presentation.

Kahneman presents another example along these lines. Kahneman asks, which of the following is true:

Adolf Hitler was born in 1892.

Adolf Hitler was born in 1887.

Trick question. Neither statement is true - he was born in 1889. More people believe the bold statement to be true than the normal font. Hence, people are more likely to believe a bold font than a normal font. Color can also affect believability. Text printed with shades of green, yellow, or pale blue are less likely to be believed than text printed with bright blue or red font.

And if bold font and font color affect believability, you might also suspect that the font itself influences believability. In 2012, Errol Morris, a filmmaker, ran an opinion piece on the *New York Times* website (Morris, 7-9-2012) and asked readers whether they believed "we live in an era of unprecedented safety?" They could choose "yes" or "no" and how confident they were in the conclusion: slightly confident, moderately confident, or very confident. Approximately 45,000 readers responded. Approximately 61% agreed with the statement and were optimists. It turns out the poll was a ruse, as reported a month later (Morris, 8-8-2012). Morris had a programmer friend of his at the Times change the font of the question each time the web page loaded. The real reason for the poll was to determine whether the choice of font influenced how confident people were in their opinions. Six different fonts were used (the font names that follow are in the actual font): Baskerville, **Comic Sans**, Computer Modern, Georgia (the typeface of the New York Times), Helvetica, and **Trebuchet**. The data were analyzed by Psychologist David Dunning at Cornell University and concluded that people who read the question with the Baskerville font had the highest rate of agreement (p=0.0068). When asked why Baskerville may have been seen as more trustworthy,

Dunning speculated that some fonts are informal, like Comic Sans, and some are "tuxedo" like Georgia and Computer Modern. Baskerville, he felt, was more formal and may have added to its level of authority.

Comic Sans font deserves some particular attention because of its notoriety and because it had the lowest rate of agreement and one of the highest rates of disagreement in the survey. The survey results regarding Comic Sans was not entirely surprising to Morris because anecdotal evidence has suggested that Comic Sans was too lightweight to be taken seriously and could render things ineffective. To illustrate this Morris provides an interesting anecdote. In July 2011 when CERN, the European Organization for Nuclear Research, reported evidence for the discovery of the Higgs Boson their press release was in Comic Sans font.[9] The choice of font caused quite a controversy in that such an undignified font was used to mark such a historic occasion. People on Twitter went ballistic and said things like "Every time you use Comic Sans on a [sic] PowerPoint, God kills Schrödinger's cat. Please think of the cat." or "They used Comic Sans on the Higgs boson [sic] PowerPoint presentation ... Nope there is no hope for mankind." Comic Sans apparently has quite a bad reputation among graphic designers and, believe it or not, there is an actual petition movement trying to ban its use (http://bancomicsans.com/).

What is the take-home message from all this? Seemingly innocuous choices like choice of font, color, or shading, are not so innocent after all and can impact our message and its believability. Kahneman refers to these as Truth Illusions - illusions that cause people to believe something even though they do not directly affect their veracity.

Another type of Truth Illusion is repetition. If you repeat something enough times it will become true. People crave the familiar. New things introduce cognitive strain. Repetition reduces cognitive strain making things seem familiar, even if they are untrue, and familiarity is the

---

[9] It turns out that Fabiola Gionatti, who wrote the press release for CERN, when asked why she chose Comic Sans font simply said "Because I like it."

foundation for belief. When things are said over and over and over, and an idea starts to sink into our brain, if we didn't initially believe the idea we may start question our beliefs and if we did believe the idea initially, it affirms our belief. This is because familiarity primes System 1 and System 1 believes something as true when it hears it over and over again. People have taken advantage of this fact for decades. Many in society have associated autism with vaccination. How many times did we hear that Iraq had "weapons of mass destruction" before the 2003 Invasion of Iraq? In both cases, repeating the mantra led many to conclude that it must be true. Surprisingly, after enough repetition, even if the idea is discredited, the idea is hard to dismiss. Despite scientific evidence that vaccination does not cause autism and despite evidence that Iraq did not have weapons of mass destruction there are still many that believe it to be true.

As presenters we can use repetition to our advantage. You've probably heard the old adage that if you want to get an idea through to the audience you need to say it not once, but many times. Choose those ideas that are important and consciously repeat them throughout your presentation. State the important points at the beginning of your talk, present them again in the middle in the results section, and in the conclusions.

At this point, you are probably saying to yourself, "This has all been very interesting but this section is called the Presenter's Paradox. Where's the paradox?" Throughout the book one of the main messages has been simplify and clarify. If you simplify too much, however, your audience will remain with System 1 being dominant. If you need the audience to really think and you have clarified too much, their brains may not switch to System 2. They won't activate the thinking, rational part of the brain and will stay in the impressionable, emotional part of the brain. Therein lies the paradox. How much do you simplify and yet still be complex enough so as to activate System 2? Or do you simplify and try not to activate System 2?

The paradox has no easy answer. If there was, it wouldn't be a paradox. How much you simplify depends on the complexity of the presentation and the overarching ideas from the presentation. There will be times when you may not want people to truly scrutinize every aspect of a presentation, in which case you will want to simplify and be coherent so as to not wake up System 2. There will be times when you want System 2 to be awake and examining the model and its conclusions.

There are no sure-fire ways to wake up System 2 and strategies designed to decrease the bias of System 1 have not been entirely successful. There are, however, some tricks you can try. One is to surprise the audience. Remember System 1 likes cohesion and a nice story. If you surprise them you will cause System 2 to wake up. Showing your results at the beginning of a presentation may serve this purpose because most people don't expect the results to be up-front; they expect them at the end of the presentation. By doing something that the audience doesn't expect, System 2 activates. Also, if the results themselves are surprising you get a double-whammy to really kick off System 2. If you have a long and difficult presentation, you may consider other surprises during your presentation to keep things going. Another way to surprise them is to insert some kind of shocking statement into your talk about time or money, since that tends to gets most executive's attention. For instance, suppose your company was planning a clinical study that would use 5 different dosages of a drug, but that based on the results from your modeling and simulation you could get equivalent statistical power with only 4 dosages of drug and save the company $500,000. After your proposal you could exclaim "Half-a-million dollars! That's how much we will save using this proposal." Questions to the audience are also very surprising. By stopping your presentation and asking the audience to respond to a question may also be useful to activate System 2.

Another trick to activate System 2 is to insert a plain black slide into your presentation. This is unusual. How often have you seen a black slide in a presentation? Not often, maybe even never. A black slide wakes people up. They think the projector is off. It forces them to look at you and not at your slides. Steve Jobs used this trick in almost every presentation he gave (Figure 37). On top of the black slide he often wore a black shirt. The only color on stage was his product. Your eyes were drawn to him and to that product. It was brilliant. When you move back to the data slides they will be more focused on the slide. The black slide is also good for your personally because it removes any crutch you may have been using if you tend to use your slides as a mnemonic to remember your content. Some have recommended that you end your talk with a black slide, like a curtain going down, but I personally think this is too formal, although you may think differently.

A few words of caution, though, regarding the use of black slides. Remove any black slides beforehand if you send the audience your slides as handouts. A black slide on a handout looks like a printer error. Also, don't use a black slide in a webinar because people may think their computer is on the fritz or there is something wrong with the internet or webinar. And lastly, if you do want to include a black slide, there is an option in PowerPoint that during slideshow mode if you press the letter 'B' or the space bar the screen will go black, just like inserting a black slide in your presentation. This is not recommended because sometimes it's hard to remember that at the end of a particular slide you want to make the screen black before you move onto your next slide. Too many times have I gone to the next slide and then realized I went too far and forgot to make my black slide stop. Use the black slide and you never forget where you want to pause.

You can also surprise an audience by being brutally frank with them. When you give a presentation on a model, people expect you to show them only the good things about it. Look how good the model fits the data and look how good the model predicts new data. The parameters of the model are very precise. Most don't expect a presenter to be totally up-front with them about the pros and cons of a model. When you show the audience the blemishes (yes, the model is a good fit to the data but it's overparameterized and the parameter estimates are unstable), you not only increase your credibility, you cause people to activate System 2 because blemishes and warts on a model cause cognitive dissonance. So, tell them the problems with the model – it'll be good for you and for them.

Figure 37. Steve Jobs was a master at using the black slide to force people to look at him. *Image reprinted from the Wikimedia Commons.*

Another way to activate System 2 is to provide options for people. If you have a decision that must be made, rather than a yes/no answer, reframe the choice into options. Be careful that you don't provide more than three or four options to choose from because going higher than that overwhelms the audience. There are lots of varieties of this method, such as grid analysis (which comes up with an answer by weighing different options) and decision tree analysis (which chooses an outcome based on possible outcomes). They all do the same thing which is to get people to think of options instead of relying on their intuition.

That's the problem though, isn't it? People trust their intuition. We use it everyday and most often we're right and everything goes off without a hitch. We've all made our fair share of bad decisions. Why? Because our intuition, which is really System 1, is easily distracted and prejudiced. It can be tricked and we can make judgments based on biases. Often when you stop and reflect, "Why did I make such a bad decision?" you realize it's not that you really made a bad decision, but that you might have rushed to judgment, not considered all the information available to you, or misunderstood some key piece of information. Had we really stopped and paid attention (and got System 2 up and running!) we might have made a better decision.

When we present to an audience, we want our audience to trust us. We want to keep them engaged. We want our models to be understandable and accessible. There are times when we want our presentation to be so coherent and clear that the audience never leaves System 1 and there are times when we really need the audience to think and get System 2 working. That is the Presenter's Paradox. It's a fine line and may not apply to every situation. Maybe in a presentation where a decision needs to be made based on the model we want the audience to activate System 2, but maybe at a scientific conference where we just want to share data its better for the audience to remain in System 1. As presenters we need to learn which system to activate and how much detail we need to provide to activate that system.

Rehearse Until You Can't Stand It Anymore

To practice and to rehearse often get confused. Magicians and athletes practice. Actors and performers rehearse. Practice is systematic training through repetition to improve a specific trait whereas rehearsals, which are a kind of practice, are done to make sure a performance in front of an audience goes off smoothly. It's kind of surprising how little time people put into creating their slide deck and even less time they spend in rehearsing it. It should go without saying that you need to rehearse your presentation, but few people do. Audiences know when you haven't rehearsed. They can see your mumbling and bumbling. They can sense your hesitancy, your uncertainty about what you are trying to say. They know you didn't take the presentation or the audience seriously enough.

Why don't people rehearse enough? There are lots of reasons. Some think they don't need to. They know the material well enough and can wing it. Some people simply don't have the time. My favorite is when you hear someone say something like "I don't rehearse because I want my presentation to sound fresh and spontaneous." That's just an excuse for laziness. Rehearsing a presentation doesn't rob it of naturalness. A well rehearsed presentation can be a thing of beauty. Just look at the TED talks (www.ted.com\talks). They are a joy to sit through. They have energy and passion. There are no 'ums' or 'so' or 'you know'. They flow and leave you excited. As much as I enjoy sitting through TED talks it would be wrong for me to give you the impression that scientific talks should be like TED talks. They can't. Presenting data takes time. There are starts and stops as people have questions. TED talks often deal with lofty goals and ideas. Modeling talks deal with data and math and science. They simply don't lend themselves to a TED-type talk. On the other hand, I am not advocating your talk must be boring. There is nothing that says in the name of science your talk can't have excitement and be interesting.

How should you rehearse? Sitting at your computer mumbling through your presentation to yourself as your flip through your slide deck or looking at your notes just prior to your presentation is not rehearsing. Actually standing up and saying aloud what you intend to say is a rehearsal. Its best to be able to rehearse in the room in which you will be speaking. You will be able to see the room's layout, where it may be best to stand and present. You can see if the acoustics are okay. You can see how the lighting is. You can see what projection equipment is available. Do you need to adjust your font size because the screen is too small to read? Many times, though, rehearsing in the room or stand-up rehearsals are not possible. I rehearse in my car while I drive to work. Granted I am not standing up but I talk to myself while I drive. I don't always start at the beginning of my presentation either because, for longer talks, I may not be able to reach the end of my talk during my commute. So, instead, I start at some random slide and proceed from there so I know what I will say at any point in my presentation. Then when I have it down, I will practice the entire presentation in my office standing up, in real time, from beginning to end. Without a rehearsal, you can't get a reliable estimate on how long your presentation will be. You won't be able to see that in one spot, you are taking too long or you are covering material too fast in another.

It's always best to rehearse in front of someone you value who will give you honest and open feedback so that you can revise and tweak your presentation if need be. If that isn't possible, then try to record your presentation as you rehearse and watch it later, maybe with an audience to get their opinion. I don't mean just record how you sound. Record your entire presentation with a video camera. Most phones today have a video camera. Use it. How do you look? Are you nervous? This is what the audience will see. Look at where you can improve and work on it. Trust me. Watching yourself a few times as you prepare will force you to become a better presenter. You know how when we record our voice and hear ourselves talk we often say "that doesn't sound like me." When you video record yourself you will often say to yourself "That was horrible. I need to practice so I don't embarrass myself."

Don't think that if you memorize your talk you will get rid of all the stumbles and errors. Memorization will kill you. If you try to stand in front of an audience and remember your presentation word for word you will fail. Any hiccup in the presentation and you will stumble when you try to get back on track. You need to learn the ideas of your presentation and the general words of what you want to say. That way if there are any problems or questions during the presentation it's easy to get back on track and into the groove of your presentation. Memorization also sounds just like that – that you memorized a script. It sounds inauthentic.

There are lots of upsides to rehearsing. First, most people don't rehearse. Because you rehearse you will be better than most other speakers and, over time, will be sought after as a speaker. Second, you will be more confident in your presentation. You will be less stressed. You will look relaxed and may actually enjoy yourself. I admit, I've given enough talks now that I actually look forward to speaking in front of an audience. I understand how an actor craves that interaction with the audience. It's electric and addictive. There also a physiological reason to rehearse. As you rehearse, your brain is forming synapses. At any given time the brain's neurons can take thousands of different paths but as you practice the number of paths reduce. You become more precise in what you want to say. If you stumble in the presentation it is easier to restart because your brain has formed those neuronal connections.

Everyone wants to give a good talk. I don't know anyone to have ever said "That stunk and am I proud of it." By rehearsing you will work out the wrinkles, you will find the places that are difficult to explain, you will get a better sense of timing, and will become more at ease about what you are presenting on so that you can focus on the audience and how they are reacting instead of reacting to how you are feeling as you give your presentation.

Concluding Remarks

Preparation is, indeed, the key to success and it begins by asking yourself what do you want from the audience? What is your key message? What do you want to happen after your presentation? By knowing these answers you can start to frame a presentation that leads the audience to where you need to take them, always keeping in mind an audience-centric, not a speaker-centric, point of view. By knowing your audience, their needs, and baseline level of knowledge you can craft an informative and understandable presentation. Using the principles described in this chapter, the five C's (consistent, clear, concise, cultured, and contents), you can prepare a presentation that will engage and inform. Once the slide deck is done you need to prepare through repeated practice. Things go awry during presentations: computers freeze, projector light bulbs go out, questions take a presentation off-topic. All of these things frazzle the less-prepared presenter and derail an otherwise engaging presentation. By rehearsing and knowing your message you can take presentations that go haywire and bring them back on course. Even if things don't go awry, rehearsing will provide you with the confidence you need for your actual presentation. As my friend Don Berk says "when you don't rehearse, the audience watches you rehearse – not good for them or for you."

Science as a Sleeping Aid

Scientific presentations don't have to be boring. Here are five tips to become a more dynamic public speaker:

1. Learn from the masters. Watch or listen to great speeches by politicians or how great comedians work an audience. Watch their timing, how they pace their material, and how they pause to allow the audience to catch-up. Don't go lightning fast or too slow.

2. Know your material. Prior to the presentation visualize it in your mind. See your audience. Think positive: visualize your success.

3. Look at your audience and smile. Eye contact is crucial for trust. Smiling helps you relax and helps you gain trust.

4. Relax. It's not life or death. It's just a presentation. It's okay to make mistakes – just look at U.S. Vice-President Joe Biden. The audience wants you to succeed. They want to learn from you. That's why you're there.

5. Practice your voice. Someone once said that monotony is a deadly sin of public speaking. Learn to modulate the volume and tone of your voice to keep the audience's attention. Learn to speak clearly without saying "um" or having verbal pauses. Remember that sometimes how you say it is more important than what you say. Drink a glass of water (avoid carbonated drinks) at room temperature 20 minutes before your talk to lubricate your vocal cords and help prevent dry mouth; it also helps you relax.

– Six –
The Big Day

It's here. The big day. The day of your presentation. You've prepared your slides. You've practiced. Aristotle spoke of Ethos, Pathos, and Logos, but what he didn't talk about was the actual physical act of giving your speech to an audience. Up to now the focus has been on Aristotle's three elements, but today you need to actually stand and deliver because today is the day you give your presentation. The strongest and most persuasive message won't matter without a strong delivery of the material

Many people though when they stand in front of an audience experience glossophobia – the fear of public speaking. If you don't get it, that's fantastic, but if you do have it, you're in good company. Thomas Jefferson, writer of the Declaration of Independence and second President of the United States, was terrified of public speaking. John Adams said that "During the whole time I sat with him in Congress, I never heard him utter three sentences together" and as President he only spoke in public twice, at both of his inaugural addresses, "in a tone so low few heard it." Some people lose sleep over it. Careers are derailed from it. At least 75% of people experience some form of anxiety or nervousness when we speak in public. Jerry Seinfeld once said "I read a thing that actually says that speaking in front of a crowd is considered the number one fear of the average person. I found that amazing – number two was death! That means to the average person if you have to be at a funeral, you would rather be in the casket than doing the eulogy."

Why? Why are people so afraid of public speaking? There are lots of reasons: fear of failure, self-doubt, fear of being mocked or laughed at, stress, fear of not being perfect, and fear of other people judging you. I think the biggest reason is 'they don't know how.' I can only remember only once or twice when I had to give a verbal presentation in college and when I was in graduate school the only training I received on public speaking was the once-a-year seminar we had to give to the faculty and other graduate students. All total I think I did four or five presentations throughout my entire graduate school experience. Today, I give four or five presentations a week, sometimes that many in one day.

When you look at books on how to give presentations, they inevitably focus on one thing - presenting to large audiences. In science, presenting to large audiences is actually not that common. You might get invited to give a seminar at a local or national meeting, but more often than not scientists present to smaller groups, like project teams, or to groups were there are a few influential decision makers. This chapter is broken down into speaking to these three groups: large audiences, medium to small audiences, and to influential decision makers, because you will give your presentations differently to these three groups. The chapter will conclude by discussing how to give a virtual presentation, when you cannot physically speak to everyone in the same room.

Presenting to Large Audiences

Large audiences can vary in size. In my view, speaking to a group that would not fit comfortably into a medium size conference room would be considered a large audience. Examples include giving presentations in an auditorium or hotel ballroom. I would even include giving a classroom

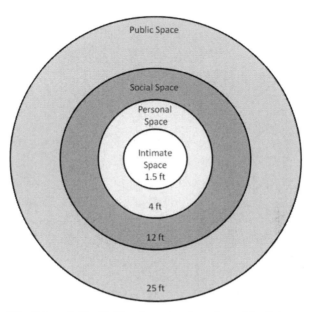

Figure 38. Edward T. Hall's four levels of social distance. *Image modified from Wikipedia (http://en.wikipedia.org/wiki/Proxemics, accessed 1 October, 2014).*

lecture in this category. Being a model communicator means being able to speak comfortably in front of any audience, no matter what the size. So whether you speak to a room full of hundreds, a conference room of 10, or even to a single person you need to be able to confidently present your material.

How you present, though, will be different depending on the size of the audience. You wouldn't expect to give the same presentation to a large group as you would to a small group. Why? Because of differences in intimacy. I don't mean like romantic intimacy. I mean personal intimacy. As the size of the audience increases, the distance from the audience to the speaker tends to also increase. Psychologists refer to this as proxemics (Figure 38). It's not unusual to see a distance of 20 feet or more between speaker and audience in a large audience setting. There is also an inverse relationship between audience size and formality – the larger the audience, the more formal the presentation tends to be. Hence, you are frequently on a stage with large audiences, often behind a podium, having to use a microphone. Your slides are projected onto a huge screen. This is a very different situation compared to a small audience where you may be just across the table from your audience and where the interaction is more personal and less formal in nature.

For some people, it's not the size of the crowd, but the distance from the audience that makes them uncomfortable. For some, it is the distance and the fact that a large crowd is staring right at them. Because of the distance between speaker and audience presentations tend to be more formal and detached. It's hard to form that personal relationship needed to make an emotional connection necessary for a successful presentation.

Not all groups are the same. Groups are fluid. They don't all have the same dynamic. Some have positive energy. Some have negative energy. It's important for you to understand what you are getting into when you step on that stage to speak. If the energy is positive, the crowd is more forgiving for mistakes, they are more positive towards what you have to say, and it's an easier experience for you. On the other hand, if the crowd is negative, you can be in for a long talk and will have to work that much harder to get the crowd to connect to you and your presentation.

Are there things you can do to facilitate an emotional connection? Certainly. One thing is to not appear nervous. Notice I didn't say "don't be nervous." I said "don't appear nervous." There's a difference. Being nervous is natural, the trick is to not be overcome by it. So what can you do to overcome your nervousness? Early in my career, before public speaking became easier for me, I used to listen to stand-up comedians on my Walkman (I know I am dating myself here). They would make me laugh and laughter always releases anxiety. I would sometimes listen to music but I found that this didn't always work, probably because the rock music I listened to didn't exactly calm my nerves. Doing things like listening to music or stand-up comics is a form of relaxation therapy. What worked for me, though, might not work for you. You need to find your own relaxation method, be it yoga, meditation, or whatever. Find something that will relax you before you get on the stage.

As an aside, going back to the stand-up comics, professional stand-up comics are brilliant presenters. Why? Because they do it every night, in front of different audiences, and they learn to overcome their nervousness. They get used to the embarrassment and they learn timing and how to read the audience. Sometime in the future watch a stand-up comic on the television or internet. Don't watch for the jokes; watch how they present. Notice their timing, notice their patterns, and pay attention to how they react to their audience. A great presenter does the same thing. They practice over and over, they start strong and get the audience laughing, they read the audience, they learn to pause at appropriate times for the audience to react to their message, and they learn to close strong "to keep them wanting more."

Earlier in the chapter on trust, I discussed ways that may increase trust the audience has in you once you are on stage presenting. This included things like body language (don't forget to smile, relax, etc.) and how you dress. There are other things that can be done as well. You might tell a personal story relevant to your presentation. Making an audience laugh is one way to turn around negative emotional energy (at least for a bit). If it isn't relevant, though, I wouldn't suggest it unless it's really funny. You can also take an interest in the audience. If everyone is tired and it's been a long day of presentations, acknowledge it. Something like "I know its been a long day of presentations but I will be succinct" will get the audience to appreciate you because you showed you care. Or if you are presenting at a conference you can say something like "How many saw the presentation on X yesterday? That got me thinking about my presentation today and how... ." In this manner you connect to the audience not just as a speaker but as an attendee as well.

When they prepare their presentation many people focus exclusively on the content of what they will present and ignore how it will be said. The vocal cadence you use is important for setting the tone of your presentation

(Chambers, 2001). If you speak too softly it suggests a lack of confidence, while if you speak too loudly it can be perceived as aggressive. If you speak too fast you can be perceived as being panicked. If you are too slow, it may be boring to some. If your tone is high pitched you may be perceived as being excited or anxious, but if your tone is low and well moderated you will be perceived as being in control and showing confidence. As you speak, vary the speed and pitch of your presentation. Pausing occasionally adds importance to your last point and gives the audience time to process what you just said. Raising or lowering your voice can emphasize a point. Always, always work to stop saying the dreaded "um's" or other crutch phrases.

Make sure the whole room can hear you. This may seem evident but I can't tell you how many times I've been to a presentation where the speaker thought they didn't need the microphone, so they refused to use it and instead gave their talk with their natural voice. Of course, those in the back of room could not hear everything that was said. So if there is a microphone, use it. Better to be heard by everyone than by only those up close.

It's also important to look at your audience. As a speaker standing on a stage facing the audience it's hard not to look at your audience, but it's easy to look out at an audience and never really see them. You can just sweep across the room never making eye contact with them. When I say look at them, I mean really look at them. Make eye contact with someone and hold it until your point is made. Don't keep looking at the same person throughout your talk. Go from person to person and maintain eye contact as you present your talking points. This helps to form an emotional connection to the audience. Even if you don't form eye contact with everyone in the audience, the audience can see you are making eye contact with audience members and this will help facilitate trust formation.

One thing that I found to be particularly effective is that when you are presenting to an audience with a nationality different than your own, you could consider trying to speak your introduction in their language. I once gave a talk to the Korean-American Pharmaceutical Scientists Association. I had a graduate student at the time who happened to be Korean. I asked her to phonetically translate my introductory remarks where I introduce myself and thank them for inviting me to speak. I practiced those few sentences over and over until I got it right. On the night of my presentation, when I stood up and spoke, they were stunned. No American scientist had ever spoken to them in Korean before. Granted my Korean was horrible, but for a few moments they thought I would try to give my whole talk in Korean. Of course I didn't, but they were so impressed by my effort that afterwards many audience members came up to me and thanked me for trying.

Most presentations to large audiences often have a podium on the stage. Many books advocate getting out from behind the podium and moving about on the stage. They suggest that some people use the podium like a shield to hide behind and protect themselves from the audience or that some people get anxious just standing behind a podium and that moving away from it will alleviate that anxiety. I have mixed feelings about this recommendation. For some people the podium alleviates anxiety. It allows them to get over their presentation anxiety. Sometimes you can't move from the podium. There may be only one microphone that is fixed on the podium. In that case, there is no option for movement. If the microphone is wireless and can be used remotely then you need to consider the environment and how comfortable you are away from the podium. Some people are better behind a podium, others are not. Dr. Martin Luther King was dynamic behind a podium, Steve Jobs was dynamic without one. How much do you want to stand out by doing something different than the other speakers? If memorable is what you are looking for this may be one way to get it. If you do move away from the podium you still need to solve the problem of going through your slides as you move about the stage. This requires someone else controlling the slide deck or some form of wireless transmitter that can control the computer which the organizers may not have. When I travel to conferences I often bring my own wireless transmitter. Before my presentation, as I am loading my slides on the presentation computer, I very nonchalantly slip the receiver into a side

USB port and that allows me to present my slides wirelessly and not be tied to the computer and podium.

If you do have to use a podium there are things you should do and things you shouldn't do. Stand straight and keep your feet planted. Don't sway or rock on stage behind the podium. Don't tap your feet. Try to look relaxed. If the podium is too tall for you then try to adjust the microphone to the side of the podium so you can stand off to its side. Make sure you know how to move through your slides on the computer before your presentation. I've sat through many presentations where the presenter gets started and then realizes they don't know where the 'page up' or 'page down' key is on this particular keyboard and they fumble about like an amateur for a few moments until they figure it out.

What I am about to suggest may seem obvious but it's worth stating: don't do something stupid as you present. There's a metaphor about 'falling into the orchestra pit.' An orchestra does this amazing concert but then at the end the conductor falls into the orchestra pit. What does the audience remember? That's right. The conductor falling; not the concert. It's easy to do something stupid on stage that can completely distract from your presentation. In 2012, Marco Rubio, the senator from Florida, was asked to give the Republican rebuttal to President Barack Obama's State of the Union Address (you can see the video on YouTube by searching Mario Rubio Pauses for Water Break). Shortly into his talk he started touching his face, licking his lips, and then he did something really weird. He reached for a bottle of water. It wasn't that he needed some water that was weird, it was how he reached for it (Figure 39). Rubio tries to bend over and keep his eyes on the camera. It was awkward and distracting. When his speech was over, did the pundits and press talk about his message? No, they spent days talking about how he tried to get a sip of water. His message was completely lost. If he had simply said "Excuse me. I need a sip of water" and then did it, there would have been no story. Instead, he did something stupid that distracted from his message. The moral of this story is "don't fall into the orchestra pit."

Figure 39. A take from the Marco Rubio School of What Not To Do While Presenting on National Television.

Also, make sure your cell phone is turned off. Some ringtones are quite funny. It could be embarrassing if your James Brown ringtone playing *Superbad* goes off during your presentation when someone calls you on your phone. I remember a few years ago I was watching this television show called America's Got Talent, which is essentially a talent show where the winner could win a million dollars. During the live portion of the show, right in the middle of someone's act, their phone went off. Rather than turn it off and continue with the act, he actually stopped, answered the phone, and told them "no, I can't talk now. I'm right in the middle of America's Got Talent." Needless to say, that individual was not asked to return the next week.

When you are finished presenting, whether it's before a large audience or a small group, don't forget to thank your collaborators or at least acknowledge their work on the project. Don't ever take sole credit for work that was a team effort. You don't have to do this at the end of the presentation, though most often this is when it is done, it can also be done at the beginning of the talk or even during the talk when different data are presented. Your collaborators will appreciate the acknowledgment and the audience will appreciate it as well.

Presenting in front of large audiences doesn't have to be scary. It can be exhilarating. I understand now why some people do theatre or stand-up comedy. The interaction with the audience can be addictive. You're living in the moment with all eyes upon you and whether you fail or succeed is entirely up to you. For some people, though, that pressure is too much and they never get comfortable speaking in public. For others, though, they embrace it. Those are the speakers who get invited again and again to speak at conferences. Those are the ones who are recognized at the workplace. Those are the ones who succeed in their careers.

Presenting to Medium and Small Groups

Medium to small-sized groups refer to audiences that can fit into a medium size conference room, about 20 people or less. Under these conditions the audience is close to the speaker, sometimes just a few feet away, and the level of intimacy between speaker and audience is immediate (Figure 38). By far most presentations are made in this setting so it's important to learn how to present under these conditions.

There are a number of differences between speaking to large audiences and speaking to smaller groups. First, the purpose of speaking to smaller groups varies more and can range from presenting data to trying to come to a decision around some issue. This differs from presenting to a large audience where the goal is usually to present information. Second, by their nature, presentations made to medium and small groups are more interactive. Presentations can start and stop as questions are asked by the audience. Because the presentations are more interactive there is less pressure for you to be the center of attention. Third, in contrast to large audiences where the vibe is often formal, the vibe with a smaller group can be formal or informal, depending on your relationship to the audience, which may influence whether you stand or sit, whether you walk the room or remain stationary, or speak formally or informally.

Figure 40. During your presentation, should you sit or stand? Where should you sit? Choosing the wrong thing can lead to awkwardness. *Image reprinted from Wikimedia Commons.*

Presentations to medium or small sized groups can be awkward. Should you sit or stand? If you sit, where should you sit? If you stand, where should you stand? Should you walk the room? Do the wrong thing and it can be embarrassing. So what should you do? The first question you should ask yourself is whether you want to be the center of attention. Suppose the room is organized as in Figure 40. In a formal presentation you want the audience to look at you so you need to stand near the screen where your slides will be shown. Sure you want the audience to look at your slides, but you also want the audience to look at you. This will have the effect of holding their attention better. If you stand facing the screen, you want to stand to the left of the screen looking at the audience as you present because since we read from left to right its natural for the audience to look at you and then read a slide. If you are standing to the right of the screen, the audience looks at you then their eyes jump to the left of the screen to start reading the slide. It's not smooth. If you are standing it's okay to move around the room.

If need be you can move the table arrangement to have greater interaction with the audience or to the sides of the room if need be but don't pace around the front of the room. Stand upright but in a comfortable position.

As you stand there be aware of the many things you shouldn't do: don't slouch, don't rock on your feet, don't sway back and forth, don't play with your keys in your pocket, don't play with your jewelry or your hair, and don't chew gum. Don't do anything that will distract the audience from you and your message or be annoying to the audience.

Standing at the front of the room also has the advantage that you can see the audience as you present. You can gauge how they are reacting to your presentation. Are they nodding off? Are they reading email? Or are they focusing on what you have to say? You may need to modify the rate and tone of your presentation to keep their attention. An important point to remember is that as you stand there, try not to look at your slides all the time; keep the audience from seeing your back.

In a less formal presentation you don't have to stand. You can sit, but, where should you sit? That's actually a complicated question. Returning to Figure 40, ideally you should sit near the front of the room by the screen, again to the left of the screen, just like if you were standing, and then talk to the audience as they look at your slides on the screen. One thing that tends to happen, though, when you sit during your presentation is that you stop looking at the audience as you speak and instead look at your slides on the screen as you talk. When this happens you wind up talking to the screen, not to the audience. Hopefully though if you are aware that this might happen you can work to prevent it. As an alternative you could sit in the back of the room so that you are looking forward towards the audience and the slides. If you do this, everyone will look at the slides and not look at you very often. You may want this. It may draw less attention to you and more attention to your slides. You need to decide what is important to you – you and your slides or just your slides. Whatever you do, though, I wouldn't recommend sitting in the middle side of the conference table or in the corners. It's hard for everyone to see you and it's hard for you to see them. It's also harder for you to project your voice to everyone in the room.

What if you have a conference room table that is more traditional where people can sit on both sides and at the end (as follows)?

First, don't take the seat at the head of the table (gray circle) unless you are the person leading the meeting or are offered to sit there by the leader. If you need to stand, it's best to stand in the front by Seat 4 for the same reasons as described previously. If you sit, you should choose Seat 4 if you want more attention directed towards you or Seats 1 or 8 if you want more emphasis on your slides. If you come with a group to give a presentation, not everyone in your group should sit on the same side of the table, i.e., Seats 1 to 4. Mix it up with people from the group on both sides of the table. The exception to this is that in some cultures, like in Japan, they may want your group to sit on one side of the table while they sit on the other side of the table.

Many of the same recommendations for large groups apply to medium and small groups. Dress appropriately. Remember your body language. Make eye contact. Maintain proper voice control. Don't do anything stupid, awkward or distracting. Keep your poise, and look and act professional. Remember that you are thoroughly prepared and that you know your material better than anyone. Although anything can happen when you present, by remaining cool and confident during your presentation, and even if things do go awry, you will be rewarded with a successful presentation.

Presenting to an Individual: Taming the HIPPOs

For any audience to buy your model, whether it is a large group, a small group, or a single person, three things must be met: trust, understanding,

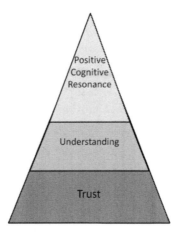

Figure 41. Successful presentations are built on trust, understanding, and positive cognitive resonance (Maurer, 2002). The audience has to trust you, has to understand you, and has to like what you have to say before they will buy what you are selling. Maurer's triangle can be thought of as a modern day re-interpretation of Aristotle's Pillars.

and positive cognitive resonance (Figure 41). Trust, the first component, has been highlighted in an earlier chapter and won't be discussed again other than to reiterate the main point – from trust all else flows. Without trust, nothing you do will get them to buy your model. The second component, understanding, is being able to grasp and comprehend the presentation. Focusing exclusively on improving understanding during a presentation is good but it is only one component for success. Positive cognitive resonance is the component most people ignore in their presentations and the one they least understand. Positive cognitive resonance has to do with generating positive emotional reactions to your ideas. Great music when heard resonates with an individual. It stays with them. They think about it. They hum it. It echoes in their head. Similarly, your presentation should positively resonate in the mind of the audience. It should cause them to feel good about what you are presenting because when a person doesn't like an idea they will be less likely to be supportive of it. I think positive cognitive resonance is best understood by understanding its opposite – negative cognitive resonance. When your ideas do not resonate with an audience, when the audience doesn't agree with what you are saying, getting them to accept your ideas is difficult.

A key aspect to any presentation is tailoring it to meet the needs of your audience as this will facilitate understanding of the model, its results, and its implications. The presentation you make for a large audience may or may not be the same presentation you make for a smaller audience but it definitely will not be the same presentation you make for a key decision maker (KDM). Remember, we want to sell our models. In a small group with a KDM, it's only the KDM who is buying. It helps to get others in a room to buy your model, but ultimately it's only the KDM who matters. Hence, the presentation you make for a KDM should be tailored to that individual.

Why does this matter? Why should you tailor your presentation to the KDM? Because how many times has the following happened to you? You go to your boss and present your work. You have everything you need in the presentation. You've got the data summary, the model, the parameter estimates, the goodness-of-fit diagnostics, the validation, and the simulation results. In the middle of your presentation, your boss starts to focus on a single graph and you spend the remainder of the time discussing that one graph, never even getting to the main point you wanted to discuss, or afterwards they say "I don't know. Let's table this for a while and discuss it again later with the rest of the team." Presentations may get hijacked by side conversations, or spend an inordinate amount of time focusing on minor details, or your boss may cut you off in the middle of your presentation and say "get to the point." You can present the same presentation to different people and they will have different reactions to it. By the same token, if you adjust your presentation to the KDM you can dramatically improve your chance of success.

Who is the KDM in a meeting? Sometimes it's obvious, but other times it's not so obvious. In my field, drug development, you may think the Project Team Leader is the KDM, but in fact, it is often the Global Medical Lead

Figure 42. Beware of HIPPOs (the HIghest Paid Person's Opinion) who can easily derail your presentation. HIPPOs can say 'no' even after everyone else has said 'yes.' *Image reprinted from Wikimedia Commons.*

(the physician) on the project that is the KDM. It's their call on what studies to do, how they should be designed, what are the endpoints, etc. Identifying the KDM may be difficult, but you can usually identify them based on who listens to whom. When someone talks does everyone pay attention and stop what they were doing? That person doing the talking is often the KDM, although this is not a foolproof rule.

Sometimes it's easy to know who the KDM is. Often times it is the highest paid person in the room. When it's their opinion that matters we call this person the HIPPO[10], for the HIghest Paid Person's Opinion. Consider this situation. You've spent months modeling some data, weeks making the presentation, and you finally get your shot to present your results to the boss. Based on the results of your model, you predict that a study the company plans to spend millions of dollars on later this year has only a small chance of succeeding. You think resources would be better spent on other studies with a greater chance of success. You make your presentation. The project team agrees with you. At the last minute, a HIPPO walks in, spends 10 minutes listening to you, and says "No. I don't

---

[10] HIPPO was first coined by Jim Sterne, a web metrics expert, in 2010 at the Neilsen Norman Group's usability conference in San Francisco.

trust models." That is that. The study continues as planned and all your work being for naught.

When there is a HIPPO in the room, you have to tame them. Otherwise there is a risk of them overruling you and your ideas even when they may not fully understand the work and the models behind your results and recommendations. How do you tame your HIPPO? Most HIPPOs have a specific style for how they like to see data presented to them. Some want high-level overviews. Some want detail, as much detail as you can give. Some want very straightforward arguments. Some only listen to proven methods. You can't give a one-size-fits-all approach to your presentations. The basic idea is to first learn what type of decision-making style the HIPPO uses and then adjust your presentation to suit their needs. However, that only gets you so far. Most people focus on the presentation, making sure the HIPPO understands the problem, the methods, the solutions, and the conclusions. The second part to taming the HIPPO is to get your idea to resonate with them. If you only focus on how things were done, you fail to show them why it should matter to them. This second step may be more important than the first step.

If you know what style your HIPPO likes to see, you can tailor your presentations to them and better enhance communication between yourself and the HIPPO. The method that I will focus on was developed by Gary A. Williams and Robert B. Miller, CEO and chairman, respectively, of Miller-Williams Incorporated, a customer-based research agency, and was reported in Harvard Business Review (Williams and Miller, 2002) and later in their book, *The 5 Paths to Persuasion* (Miller and Williams, 2004). What follows is a review of these two resources. In a 2-year study of more than 1,684 executives (defined as vice-president or above), Williams and Miller interviewed and examined how the executives in a variety of different industries made their decisions. Questions ranged from how long it took for them to make a decision to how willing they were to make a decision that might have negative consequences to them or the company. The industries they studied included automotive, software, consulting, consumer durables, apparel, technology, telecommunications, retail, and services.

Williams and Miller found that executives tend have a dominant decision-making style when they have to make tough decisions. Using cluster analysis they were able to classify these decision-making styles into five different categories, which they labeled as charismatics, controllers, followers, skeptics, and thinkers. They are not saying that every executive uses a single decision-making style for every decision, but that they tend to favor one specific style and that knowing how they make their decisions can help you in your presentation by tailoring your presentation to better fit their style. I personally have used this system for more than 10 years and can say that I have had some remarkable successes by adjusting my presentation to my HIPPO. Each of these categories will now be discussed in turn.

Charismatics, which accounted for a quarter of the executives studied, are the easiest to spot. I tend to think of this group as the executives with ADHD. They have short attention spans and don't like long, boring presentations. They move rapidly from idea to idea. They like big ideas, are known as big picture people, and focus on the bottom line. They have no problem with analysis paralysis and make bold decisions, but they also tend to have a number two person behind them who can act to kill bad ideas. They tend to be visual in how they process information and don't like numbers. In fact, they tend to take pride in that they don't like numbers. In a sense they are just what the label says – they are charismatic in nature. They are innovators and the mavericks of their field. They are enthusiastic, talkative, captivating, and persistent. When they are in a room, they dominate the conversation. One example of a charismatic is Sir Richard Branson, who has said it took him years to learn the difference between 'net' and 'gross,' is known to be a quick decision maker and has so many ideas he has a notebook to keep track of them. Oprah Winfrey, another charismatic, says she is functionally illiterate in math and technology, and is yet one of the largest media moguls on the planet.

Figure 43: All executives tend to rely on a single, dominant decision-making style when they have tough decisions to make. Knowing that style can help you tailor your presentation and increase your chances for a successful outcome. *Images reprinted from Wikimedia Commons.*

When presenting to a charismatic don't present a ton of information. Keep your slides to the bare minimum. Use headlines to grab their attention. Start off with the most important parts of the presentation. Focus on the big ideas and bottom-line results but be balanced in your arguments, be honest, and be open as they are quick to spot one-sided arguments. Be very visual in your presentation. Be as simple and straightforward as possible. If you are not an enthusiastic presenter, you might consider having someone else from the modeling team present the results if they are more kinetic than you. If you start to lose their attention, they will quickly interrupt you and ask you to get to the point. Be prepared for aggressive questioning throughout the presentation and afterwards because charismatics want to make sure that, even though they don't want to know the model particulars, they want to make sure that any data or model was thoroughly analyzed.

Controllers, the smallest group accounted for 9% of executives studied, hate the unknown and have to be in charge of all aspects of decision-making. They are detail-oriented, analytical, and crave information because

169

of their fear and insecurities about how their decision might affect them or the company. They are constantly looking for more information as if some new piece of information will grant them the peace of mind they need in making their decision. As such, they are constant worriers and take an inordinate amount of time to make a decision. Surprisingly, even though controllers want information they may not use it since they tend to trust themselves and their ability to make a decision. Tough-minded, persistent, and unyielding, controllers are extremely rigid with regard to how they think things should be done because their opinion is the only one they truly trust. They can be overbearing and micromanage situations to the point where they lose sight of the objective. Because of their style, controllers are either loved or hated by their staff. Examples of controllers include Martha Stewart and George Steinbrenner. Martha Stewart once described herself as a "maniacal micromanager" who needed to understand "every part of the business to be able to maximize those businesses." George Steinbrenner's micromanagement of the New York Yankees baseball team is legendary even going to the point where he dictated how his baseball players would cut their hair. It can be argued whether their controlling nature contributed to their success but in their minds it was.

When presenting to a controller you need to allay their fears and prepare yourself for a long road ahead. Make them feel that the model is the only solution to the problem but don't be too pushy because controllers hate people who try to force a decision. You need to use well-structured, linear, detailed arguments presented by an expert with credibility. Check and double-check your presentation for accuracy. Mistakes will only increase their fear and decrease your credibility, even if it's something stupid like a typographical error on a slide. If you are a junior modeler, you would be better served to have your data presented by a more senior staff member or collaborator than to present it yourself. Because controllers operate from a place of fear they can be quite emotional and at times angry so the best thing you can do is to remain as calm and in control as possible. Getting emotional with a controller only makes things worse. Unfortunately, you can never really persuade a controller of anything, they only persuade themselves, so if you can include the controller to take part of the model building process, do so as much as possible to give them a sense of ownership.

Followers, the largest group, accounted for more than a third of executives studied, are traditionalists and make decisions based on what has worked for them in the past or what others have successfully done. Followers are not looking for the best solution; they are looking for a safe solution. For them, a safe solution is one that has been shown to work before. Hence, they are good corporate citizens who protect and maintain a business and will work to maintain the status quo. It's easy to see why followers are the largest group because they are not risk-takers, innovators, or adopters of new technology. In a corporate environment not being a risk-taker is a useful strategy because risk-takers swing for the fences and either fail or succeed. Followers are happy with just getting on base (apologies for my baseball metaphors). After all, not everyone needs to be an innovator. In certain industries, like the military or insurance industry, there is a strong motivation to maintain the status quo.

Examples of followers can be found in descriptions of Hollywood studio bosses. It's hard to get the approval for a movie based on a new, original concept. Instead, it's much safer to approve a movie based on some other movie or, better yet, a sequel to a previously made movie. This is why there are 7 sequels to the Fast and the Furious (as of 2013). To get original movies made, writers and pitchmen need to come up with a catchy tagline that says how the movie they want to make is like another hit movie. For example, the movie Alien (1979) was pitched as "Jaws in Space," a reference to the blockbuster movie Jaws made a few years earlier. Chip and Dan Heath, in their book *Made to Stick* (2008), call this anchoring and twist, the process of tying an idea to another existing idea (anchoring) and then differentiating it into something else (twisting). Other specific examples of followers in the business world include Carly Fiorina, who was CEO of Hewlett-Packard from 1999-2005, and Ron Johnson, who was CEO of JC Penney department stores from 2011-2013. Rather than being seen as innovation, Fiorina's merger of Hewlett-Packard and Compaq was viewed as a tired merger of equals much like the merger of Exxon-Mobil a decade earlier. Johnson came from Apple where he was Senior Vice President of Operations. He was responsible for turning Apple stores into fun stores with lots of gadgets. At JC Penney, he initiated a virtual overnight transformation and rebranding of the store. Using the same ideas used by Apple, he applied it to JC Penney, which in this case resulted in a disaster for the company. He was fired in less than 2 years.

When presenting to a follower you need to keep it simple and keep them in their comfort zone. Don't show them the novelty of your methods. Show them you are using tried and true methods; that you have used proven and published models that are respected and agreed upon by experts. You can include examples where a similar model was used by others. Use phrases like "a similar model was used by....," "this is like the model published by...," and "We based our model on our previous model." Followers don't necessarily want details so much as proof that the methods are proven and trusted.

Skeptics, who accounted for nearly a fifth of executives studied, are take-charge people who are inherently suspicious of data presented to them unless its presented by a credible source. They will challenge data and conclusions, especially opinions, to the point of disruption and will not believe results even when they are accurate. Their personalities are strong. They say what they want, are confident with little self-doubt, and are outspoken. You can be confident about where you stand with a skeptic because they will let you know. Because of their overconfidence they have no problem making fast decisions.

Skeptics have larger than life personas. A classic example is Ted Turner, who founded the CNN News Network and other cable channels, was owner of the Atlanta Braves, and was named Time Magazine's 1991 Man of the Year. His tendency for bold, outrageous statements earned him the nickname "Captain Outrageous" and "the Mouth of the South." He criticized cable television, of which he himself owned many channels, for its "sleaze, stupidity, and violence" and called the 10 Commandments "outmoded rules." Skeptics are determined, driven, and get results. When the U.S. boycotted the 1980 Summer Olympics, Turner started the Goodwill Games as an alternative, the last of which was held in 2005. Turner was said to remark that the cancellation of the games was "short-sighted" and had he stayed involved in the Games they would not have been canceled.

When presenting to a skeptic, the most important thing is to build credibility with them. They tend to trust people who are like them or look for people with established, solid reputations. Although they have no problem with ground-breaking ideas, and can come to a decision quickly, sometimes on the spot, ideas have to come from people they trust. If you don't have their trust, you have to find someone the skeptic does trust and get endorsement from that person. You have to get that person to transfer their credibility to you. This only goes so far because the skeptic will test you. They will challenge you and question your conclusions because they are looking for reasons not to trust you. Your presentation must be forceful, avoiding passive voice. Be ready for a constant barrage of potentially intimidating questions and comments, some of which could be about you personally. It's imperative to stand your ground and remain calm. If you outwardly challenge them back, look out, there's going to be trouble. Only as you weather their storm do you start to establish credibility with them. If you fail their test, forget it, you've lost your chance with them and building credibility with them again is near impossible.

Thinkers, who accounted for about 1 in 10 executives studied, are the nerds, the brains of the organization. They are intellectual and academic in their approach to problems. They want to see data – as much as you can present. In their review of data and models, they are methodical and precise. They want to see the parameter estimates of a model and their standard errors. They want to see all the p-values for an analysis. They review everything in a logical, orderly process and take great pride in their memory and ability to out-think others. They want to make sure they have all the information needed to make a decision. Working with a thinker can be frustrating because they like to examine both sides of an argument and have no problem reversing a decision when they are wrong.

Examples of thinkers are Bill Gates and Warren Buffett. Bill Gates used to sit in on classes at Harvard he wasn't even signed up for. At Microsoft he was notorious for his long and grueling interrogations in meetings and his decisions were always data-driven. Warren Buffett will only invest in a business he thoroughly understands. He wants to know how the company will perform in the next 20 years, so instead of investing in difficult to predict companies like software or internet companies, he invests in tried and true businesses like Coca-Cola and Heinz Ketchup.

When presenting to a thinker, give them details. Show them how you went from your starting model to the best model. Even better is to actually involve them in the modeling process. They want to know that you have been thorough and haven't overlooked anything. They want to know where the model limitations are and what the model's weak points are. They will ask lots of questions but they are doing so from a place of curiosity and intellectual satisfaction. They want to know it all. Get them involved. Ask them their suggestions for how to improve things. Ask them if they see anything you overlooked?

In order to use Williams and Miller's stylistic guide, it's all predicated on your ability to decipher the HIPPO and identify their dominant decision-making style. Most people have two or more styles they may use, but often they have one single dominant style. Choosing the wrong style can be a disaster. Imagine presenting to a charismatic as if they were a thinker. So how do you learn what style a HIPPO is? Williams and Miller recommend to first assume they are a follower (because of their chameleon-like behaviors) unless proven otherwise and then work down a flowchart-like list of questions:

1. Do they want their information presented as highlights, in bullet-point format, and do they get excited about big ideas? If so, they are likely a charismatic. If they have difficulty making a decision they are not likely to be a charismatic.

2. Are they always weighing the pros and cons of every decision? Are they methodical and very process-oriented in how they come to decisions? If so, they are a likely a thinker. If they make decisions easily on-the-spot, they are likely not a thinker.

3. Are they skeptical of everything you say? Do they say things like "Let me play devil's advocate...?" If so, they are likely a skeptic.

4. Are they involved in every decision? Do they practically micromanage you as you work through a problem? Is it difficult to get them to change their mind once they have made a decision? Do they blame others when things go wrong? If so, they are likely a controller.

5. Do they only agree with ideas that have been proven to work in the past? If so, they are a follower. If all the other questions were answered with a 'no,' they are likely a controller.

Learning someone's decision-making style is not an easy process and may take months of work with lots of interaction with the HIPPO.[11] You could start off thinking someone was a thinker and then realize they are a controller. Fortunately, it's possible to quickly discern or rule out a person's style. For example, skeptics are generally easiest to spot and you won't miscategorize a charismatic for a controller. Whatever you do, however, don't make your classification based on a single instance. You have to watch the person for their actions and not necessarily what they say. They may talk one way but decide another way entirely.

One problem with Williams and Miller's decision-making style guide is that it is decidedly Amerocentric. A total of 97% of executives studied were American and in America individual managers and groups are empowered to make decisions on behalf of the company. Under these

---

[11] One of the reviewers of this book suggested talking to the HIPPO's administrative assistant. They will know how their boss likes to see information presented to them.

Figure 44. "Nemawashi" in Japanese literally means "digging around the roots" and refers to a gardening term whereby when a tree is transplanted the gardener wraps the roots in a cloth to prepare it for transplant. Without Nemawashi the tree may die. In Japanese business, Nemawashi refers to "laying the groundwork" or building consensus before meetings. *Figure reprinted courtesy of Antonio Marques (http://www.tzplanet.com/).*

conditions, decision-making can easily be dominated by a few HIPPOs and using their style guide can be a useful influential tool. In other cultures, however, Williams and Miller's style guide may not be as useful.

If you consider individual autonomy in decision-making as a continuum, Americans are probably in the middle between two extremes, the Japanese and Chinese. Let's start with the differences between Americans and the Japanese in decision-making. In the U.S., meetings tend to be the place where ideas are pitched, disagreements and heated discussions may occur, and where decisions are made. Not so in Japan where public disagreements are anathema and decisions are largely made by group consensus prior to the meeting, a process known as "Nemawashi." No one is allowed in Japan to make decisions on their own. Japanese view meetings as a place to update information that has already been agreed upon and where decision-making is a formality.

Nemawashi is a part of everyday life in Japan. It is done informally by stopping someone in the hallway or in social settings like at a meal and telling them about your proposal. "Let me tell you about this model I am working on." Or it can be done more formally at pre-meetings which are meant to inform everyone of the model and resolve any criticisms before moving onto the next level of consensus. If your proposal meets with strong resistance you can decide not to pitch your proposal any further.

Suppose your model predicts that the probability of an expensive clinical trial succeeding is small and that you believe the study should be cancelled. In the U.S., you would make your pitch in front of senior management and they would decide whether to terminate or continue the project. In Japan, you can't just make your pitch at the meeting. To do so would cause group disharmony, which is something the Japanese avoid. Also, a manager who hears a proposal for the first time in a pitch meeting may feel that they were ignored in the Nemawashi process and may purposefully sabotage the project. To start Nemawashi with your proposal, you would first consult all the people in your department. Once they are on board with your proposal, you could then bring it to your manager. Your manager would then consult all the managers at their level and this process would continue until it reaches senior management. Then, once senior management agrees, you would have permission to have your meeting with them to make your proposal, at which time they are almost certain to agree. In this manner, ideas with a low chance of success are weeded out before the employee "loses face" (be publicly embarrassed) with senior management and ideas are improved upon as they move through the process.

Many people not familiar with Nemawashi believe that the Japanese cannot come to a decision, that decision-making is agonizingly slow, and that final decisions made in a meeting are based on some foregone conclusions and hidden agenda. Decision-making is slow (you won't ever hear someone from Japan say "Time is money" or talk about a "Window of Opportunity") but it is slow for a reason. All proposals are strongly vetted by many layers prior to ever reaching the meeting in which the decision is "made." Working to a consensus before the meeting has the advantage in that HIPPOs don't have as much influence as they do in American business meetings.

When working with the Japanese, instead of trying to sell to one HIPPO you have to sell to a number of individuals. How do you do that? About three-quarters of Japanese report that they are risk-averse and that decision-making can be a long and arduous process. Who does that sound like? A controller, right? Also, Japanese tend to look back on history as part of their decision-making process.

They don't jump onto fads but instead look for things that have been tried before and shown to be successful. Who does this sound like? A follower. In business, Japanese like to be "fast-followers" by letting others take the brunt of the risk first and then learning from their mistakes. Hence, treating the Japanese as a blend of controller and follower may be a useful strategy. You should work to understand their concerns and what aspects of your proposal make them most uncomfortable. Japanese decision makers favor decisions that maintain established relationships and do not disturb the status quo. Make sure you don't emphasize any novelty in your model. If the model is based on published literature make sure to point that out and highlight how often it has been used. If other companies have used the methodology before, you should mention that as well. Don't forget the language barrier if you are not Japanese. Make sure to use plain and simple English.

Let's assume you've made your pitch to your Japanese colleague(s). You stand there, looking at them, waiting for a "yes, that's a great idea" or "no, that idea will never work." The problem is that you may never hear your colleague say directly to you "no, that's a bad idea" because Japan is generally a conflict-avoiding society and saying "no" directly to someone is too confrontational. In my experience, though, it depends on the situation and their relationship with you as to how frank they will be. If you have a strong relationship with the person and the setting is informal, I have noticed that a direct "no" may be given, but in formal settings where you may "lose face," the Japanese won't say "no" directly to a proposal. Instead, they will find some polite way to decline a proposal that may be so polite you might not even realize you are being turned down. They might say "Let's meet again sometime to discuss this" (which may mean what they say but more often than not means "no"). They may avoid giving you feedback or may give you a vague "yes." A favorite phrase I have encountered is "it is difficult" which I have learned is code for "no," or "Sumimasen" or "Sorry," which is also code for "no." Japanese may also use body language or facial expressions to respond, such as leaning back and sucking air through their teeth which means "that's a stupid idea." In Japan it is important to "read the air" as they say for both verbal and body language cues as to the meaning of their response.

The process of nemawashi, though a decidedly Japanese concept, is a useful idea in any culture. Meeting with the HIPPO prior to your presentation can help alleviate any problems that arise during a presentation and can aid on consensus building. I remember one time I was in a meeting where we were presenting the results of a model to a group of HIPPOs. One of them hijacked the meeting and went after us because he disagreed with the modeling approach that was taken. After the meeting we went back to our desks, licked our wounds, and did some additional modeling work to alleviate the HIPPO's concerns. Before we were to meet again as a group, we met individually with the HIPPO causing us problems and with some of the other HIPPOs in the room to lay the groundwork for our next team meeting. When the next meeting came, the modeling work was accepted without any trouble.

Now let's contrast the Japanese and Americans with how the Chinese make decisions. The Chinese have what is called a high "power-distance," their willingness to accept an unequal distribution of power in society, and a low level of individualism, the degree to which they achieve their identity through their own achievements (Martinsons, 2001). In contrast, the Japanese and U.S. both have a moderate power distance but the U.S. has a much higher individualism score. The Chinese tend to be more hierarchical in their decision-making with harmony flowing from the top down. Hence, employees expect their "boss" to make the final decision and are not comfortable when they are expected to do so. Managers are seen as being "most wise" in decision-making and, indeed, will shun subordinate input in their decision-making process.

Like in the U.S., focusing on these key decision leaders in China is a good strategy for selling your models. Unlike the U.S., decision-making is still slow in China, even though decision-making is made by individuals, because the Chinese tend to look at the big picture and view an issue's complexity as a whole (Gallo, 2008). They also want to make sure that an issue is examined from all angles which may entail going over and over material that has already been covered. In fact, many Chinese view a quick decision as a kind of incompetence they can exploit when negotiating with Westerners. Further, Chinese managers look towards preserving the future when making decisions and may make a decision that is "safe" rather than cutting-edge. Just like the Japanese, the Chinese are sensitive to "losing face" and will tend to make safe decisions, but are more direct in telling you "no." Because the Chinese place a heavy emphasis on relationships, expect to spend a great deal of time building your relationship with the KDM.

In putting together a presentation, most people focus on improving clarity and increasing understanding of the material. This is just one facet of getting the HIPPO to buy what you are selling. Assuming trust is already present, the last component to a successful presentation is to give your audience a positive emotional reaction to your presentation. You want to avoid people saying afterwards "I didn't like it." How do you do that? How do you get people to like your ideas? When someone is in the audience listening to your presentation they are asking themselves questions. Certainly questions about the material but also about questions like "Will this benefit me"? "Will my boss like this idea?" "Is this good for the company?" In short, they are asking themselves "How does this affect ME?!" A negative answer to any of these questions may be enough to kill a presentation.

Figure 45. Before he became a U.S. Senator, Al Franken was a writer and member of Saturday Night Live. A running gag on the show was Al Franken asking "How does that affect me, Al Franken?" In preparing your presentation to a HIPPO you should be asking yourself "How will this affect the HIPPO?" *Image reprinted from Wikimedia Commons.*

After reading this chapter you may think that this is all baloney. Maybe so, but I can swear that using the Williams and Miller style categories works. I've had many examples where their decision-making guide has helped me in getting acceptance of my models. Once there was a senior executive at my company who was what I call an n-charismatic – a charismatic raised to the power n. He wanted to review some models we were developing. The slide deck that was prepared for him was made by someone who happened to be a thinker. Can you see the presentation disaster that is coming? That is exactly what happened. The presenter was chastised for the lack of clarity in their presentation and our department was criticized for the work. After that we went through every future presentation and clarified and simplified to the point where the presentation was a skeleton of the original. No more complaints. Another time I was working for a company where I had to routinely work with the vice-president of my division. For the first year I was convinced that they were a thinker. They were so slow and methodical in their deliberations. They were always asking for more information, more detail. Then I mentioned that the model

I used was used by one of the larger competitors in our field and like magic the gates opened up and he was receptive to my proposal. He was a follower disguised as a thinker. I needed to couch my arguments in tradition and not point out the novelty of my methodology. After that, I experienced greater acceptance of my work by him.

I've also learned to value my relationships with my Asian colleagues more as I gain a better understanding of their culture and how they make decisions. I always appreciated their politeness, but I remember being somewhat frustrated during my first year working for a Japanese company at the speed at which decisions were made and by the ambiguity in which the Japanese responded to my questions. At first I chalked the latter up to English translation issues. I've learned that difficulty in translation is sometimes part of the problem, but I now appreciate that their messages are meant to be ambiguous on purpose. It's just part of their culture. I now try to read more between the lines and appreciate our differences when we interact.

Presentation Disasters

Despite the best laid plans, things can go wrong during a presentation - sometimes spectacularly. Joan Lloyd (2014) at jobdig.com tells some great stories of presentation disasters that happened to her and her friends. One time her skirt fell off during her presentation. The button had fallen off her skirt the morning of the talk and she wasn't able to fix it in time, so she went on stage hoping the zipper would be enough to hold it in place. It wasn't and her skirt fell to the floor, revealing her slip underneath. Another time a friend of hers had a pair of underwear (not the pair she was wearing) fall from her skirt onto the stage. The underwear must have gotten caught in the skirt while doing laundry and fell out during her presentation. There are other great anecdotes she tells but fortunately most presentation disasters are more mundane like a microphone that won't turn on or a laser pointer going dead. Some, though, can be a bit more serious, like when you can't get your presentation to project onto the screen or if you are sick on the day of your talk.

How do you handle such problems? There is no one solution. You have to do what you can to solve it. You may have to talk loudly if the microphone won't turn on. Maybe you can get another laser pointer, or maybe you can use the mouse cursor on your computer as a pointer if the laser pointer dies during your talk. The point is that quick thinking will save the day. When things go bad, try not to let it throw you off your presentation, although this might be easier said than done for some people. One thing that always seems to work is that the bigger the disaster the bigger you should laugh about it. When Ms. Lloyd's skirt fell down, rather than panic and run off the stage in embarrassment, which is what she probably wanted to do, she laughed about it and said "Now that I have your attention" and she went on with her talk. Audience members are sympathetic when things go awry so a little self-deprecating humor can go a long way.

If you're sick, don't start your talk by apologizing and saying "Sorry, I'm sick." After that people will focus on your not feeling well. It's okay to start your talk and then tell people you are not feeling well. That way if you need to stop and drink something they will understand. You may want to consider drinking beforehand and during your talk some hot green or herbal tea with ginger and lemon, which is said to be useful for relaxing vocal cords. Stay away from caffeinated beverages which are said to dry out vocal cords and may prevent you from staying hydrated. A few other suggestions are to try and pace yourself, if possible sit down while you present, and consider that when your ears are plugged from congestion that you may be talking louder than normal since you can't hear yourself all that well.

Just remember, whatever happens, happens. Deal with it. Don't do what Michael Bay, director of the Transformers movies, did in front of a huge crowd at the Consumer Electronics Show in 2014 and walk off the stage, apologizing when his teleprompter stopped working. If you have adequately prepared yourself and rehearsed enough, whatever problem you face you can overcome. Be calm, act professional, work through it and you will see that it isn't the end of the world after all.

Virtual Presentations

Our workforce is becoming more and more invisible. We work globally across vast geographical distances. Even at local sites people are increasingly working from home, at least part of the time. The days of working side-by-side in the same location are over. The people we work with are, in essence, invisible. Travel budgets, which include travel to professional meetings for continuing education, are also being slashed in many companies in an effort to reduce costs. Employees don't have the benefit of always being able to attend a conference in person. Quite simply, it's becoming harder and harder to communicate with others face-to-face.

As a result of these changes, companies are increasingly relying on virtual presentations as a way for employees to cross distances and communicate. Many professional organizations are using virtual presentations to reach their members. In theory, this is great. Costs go down because people don't have to travel to meetings. Employees can work across vast distances and still interact productively. Plus, there is the potential to reach a huge audience. It's a win-win for everyone. The problem is that most people prepare for virtual presentations as an actual face-to-face presentation. Virtual presentations, though, are an entirely different beast altogether than in-person presentations. Think about it. If you are an attendee, often all you see are the slides on your computer. You don't see the actual presenter; they're just a disembodied voice over the phone or computer. If you are the presenter, you can't see the audience or get their feedback about how you are doing. Do they look bored? Do they look like the understand it? Heck if you know, you can't see them.

Because the rules of etiquette don't apply when the presenter is not in the room, often during a presentation the audience is multi-tasking doing things like checking their email or surfing the internet at the same time while you are giving your presentation. Their attention is thus divided between you and distractions. If you aren't more interesting than the distractions, what are they going to do during your talk? That's right. They aren't going to give you the same level of attention as they would otherwise give. Virtual presentations also seem cumbersome because of technological glitches that often occur: videos won't play, it takes too long to make someone a presenter, and sometimes the presentation just hangs up and won't go to the next slide.

The result is that in a survey of webinar-type presentations the one-word that described their quality 38% of the time was "suck." When I think about my past experiences with webinars I agree with this. Most of them do suck. The way I look at it, virtual presentations only make your weaknesses bigger. If you are a boring presenter, a virtual presentation makes you more boring because the audience can't see you. If your presentations are too technically complex and cause the audience to have cognitive overload the audience will stop listening to you earlier in your presentation. Language and cultural barriers are also exacerbated. The list goes on and on.

As a presenter you have to prepare your virtual presentations differently than you would if you were giving a face-to-face presentation. If you remember one thing about virtual presentations it's that you have to keep it engaging and moving. Your presentation should move along at a nice clip and not linger on any one slide for too long. You have to grab your audience from the very beginning and change your slides more frequently. If you keep a slide up for too long, people will start to wonder if there is a problem with their computer with the slide not changing. If your presentation starts to drag, that's it, you're done. You've lost them. They're going to focus on other things.

Timothy Koegel in his book *The Exceptional Presenter Goes Virtual* (2010) (which is an excellent resource and worth reading) makes a great point that is worth noting. Virtual presentations are nothing new. Think about radio and television newscasts, both of which are virtual presentations. The broadcaster has no feedback from their audience in real time to gauge how they are doing. The audience cannot interact with the broadcaster. How does the news keep their audience so they don't change the channel? They report interesting things and keep it moving. How long does a TV news story last? Not long. They keep it short, in a series of segments, and keep the audience interested. They also meticulously script how long each segment will last and organize each segment to make a complete newscast. You never see the news going over their time limit unless there is some major news event.

As a virtual presenter you too will have to rigorously organize your presentation, more so than if you were doing a face-to-face presentation, and make your slides otherwise more attractive. As you prepare, ask yourself, "How would I do this if I were doing it face-to-face?" and then ask yourself "How do I need to modify it for a virtual presentation?" For example, if you would normally spend a few minutes on a single slide, you may need to break it up into a series of different slides for a virtual presentation in order to keep the talk moving. A general rule of thumb is that virtual presentations use more slides than a face-to-face presentation. Slides should be more colorful, not over the top colorful, but a white slide with black text may not be attractive enough for a virtual presentation. Your first slide, which displays when participants log onto a presentation, acts like a banner for you and sets the tone for your talk. If it is colorful and attractive people will find it inviting. If it is boring and matter of fact, people will be less excited about what you are going to say. As an example, look at Figure 46. This slide is from a presentation I gave in 2013 at the 3rd World Cancer Online Conference using the title slide template from my company. Astellas is a Japanese-owned pharmaceutical company. Notice how the birds are like origami, Japanese paper folding, and the colors evoke a peaceful emotion to them. This slide is very inviting to the audience.

If you are going to use a technology, like Cisco WebEx or GoToMeeting, you should learn how to use it. Be aware of what its limitations are. For example, some software won't run videos within PowerPoint presentations, some meeting tools have limits on how many attendees there can be, and some meeting tools won't work on mobile phones like Blackberry or Android. Of the different meeting tool options, they all have their quirks

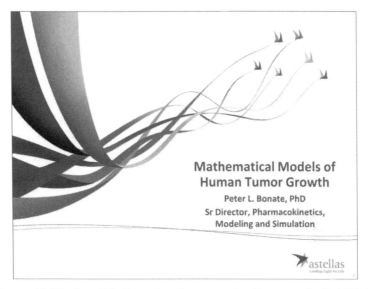

Figure 46. Display slide for a virtual presentation I gave to the 3rd World Cancer Online Conference in January 2014 using the Astellas Pharma global PowerPoint template. Note the attractiveness of the slide, which makes it appealing to the audience.

and they all have different user interfaces. If you are used to a WebEx interface don't be surprised by the interface if you now have to present with Adobe Connect. Play with the tool beforehand. Do you have to upload your slides before you present? How do you annotate during your presentation? How do you answer questions during your presentation? Does the tool offer side-by-side windows for your slides and a video of you as you give your presentation? These questions (and others) should not be answered by you as you try to figure it out during the presentation. You should know the answer to these beforehand.

I personally like those meeting tools that have the option of showing both slides and video of you and the participants at the same time within the window. This is a great way to overcome speaking into a black hole. There are issues with this though. Video uses a lot of bandwidth over the internet and you may find that the whole presentation drags when you try to use both video and your slides simultaneously. It may be necessary to limit the video to only yourself in an attempt to reduce the bandwidth drain, but even then be aware that you may have bandwidth issues. Also, if you are going to be presenting video of yourself be aware of what your picture looks like to the participants. Common problems are that too many people have their video camera too close and they appear gigantic to the audience, their video camera is too low and they are awkwardly not looking at their audience, the background behind them is distracting, or they appear to be in a science fiction movie when wearing a headset (Figure 47). I should also point out that with the new video cameras that generate 1080p video, the camera can be unforgiving with regards to skin color, bags under your eyes, and wrinkles so you may want to consider a lower resolution camera.

If you are going to use a webcam as part of your presentation, here are a few guidelines to make you look like a professional:

- Use external lighting. Good lighting is one of the differences between success and failure with using a webcam. Most offices have insufficient light to illuminate a person's face without shadow. Further, most lights are in the ceiling and cast a weird shadow on your face. Professional photographers use four lights to ensure no shadows on an object. That's not practical here, so at least make sure that the light source is in front of you and not behind you, or on the side of you. If you can't get natural light in front of you, use a lamp. Don't light yourself from below because then you start to look like some horror movie monster. What you want is the light in front of you slightly above your eyes. Do a check to make sure the light isn't too bright on your face. If it is, move it back a little.

- Make sure you have a good background. Don't have a cluttered background as it makes you look like a slob. A white wall is too plain. Have a background that looks like an office. A bookcase or a white wall with a modest picture behind you is a good choice. Try to remove any clutter from the frame – get rid of that coffee mug

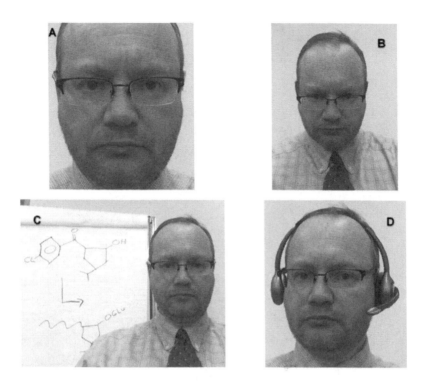

Figure 47. Things to avoid if you use your computer webcam to broadcast yourself as you give a virtual presentation.

A: "Do not arouse the wrath of the great and powerful Oz." In this setting the presenter sits too close to their camera and appears to be gigantic. There is no background, only a giant head. The lighting is also awful.

B: "Whatcha lookin' at?" In this setting the presenter is looking down at their computer screen and is not making eye contact with the audience.

C: Are those company secrets behind you? In this setting the presenter is sitting in front of a whiteboard that contains chemical structures of possible proprietary nature.

D: "Beam me up, Scotty." In this setting the presenter is wearing their Bluetooth device. While not a major mistake it's better if you can use your webcam microphone, a single-ear Bluetooth device, or an unobtrusive dual ear headset (see Figure 48).

sitting on your desk next to you, for example. Make sure the background is static and doesn't move as that can be distracting. Don't forget – you are the center of attention in the webcam, not your background or stuff around you.

- Make sure you have good sound and are in a quiet room without distracting sounds. An empty room may make you sound hollow. Rooms with "stuff" in them sound more realistic. Make sure you are close enough to the microphone that your voice sounds natural. If you need, consider an external microphone if your laptop sounds tinny or unnatural.

- Don't use your laptop camera. Use an external camera whenever possible and make sure the camera is eye-level. If you have to use your laptop camera, stack it on a box or some books to make it eye-level. You do not want your laptop camera below you while you look down towards the camera. You want your eyes to be about 2/3rd the way to the top of the frame. Be a little more than arm's length from the camera so that your face doesn't appear gigantic in the frame. And make sure you look directly or slightly up at the camera like you were talking to a person across from you. Looking directly at the camera could be problematic if your camera is on top on your monitor. Your eyes then flicker back and forth between the camera and your monitor. If possible, put your monitor behind your camera at the same height as your camera so that you stop that eye flickering going back and forth.

- Lastly, make sure you look good. Don't wear an old sweatshirt from your alma mater or crazy colored sweaters or shirts. Wear professional clothes, at least on top or at least in the camera frame. Center yourself in the frame. Given the quality of high-definition cameras, wearing make-up should not be ruled out, even for men. Make sure you are completely in frame an once the webinar starts, try not to move around too much as it can be distracting.

Figure 48. Proper technique for using a webcam. The presenter is properly illuminated, is seated at arm's length from the camera, and is looking directly into the camera, which is at eye-level. Her headset, while present, is not too obtrusive. The background is not distracting – your eyes are drawn to her. She is the center of attention in the frame.

You may need to experiment with these guidelines to find the right conditions for your webinar. See Figure 48 for an example of proper use of a webcam.

Here are a few tips for when you actually give your presentation. First, it may be useful to have a second computer running so that you can see what the audience sees. One computer will be for you to give your presentation, the other will be for you to see how things are going in real time for the audience. You can see when there is a lag between slide transitions or animations are not working properly. You can pause appropriately until the presentation catches up with you. Second, an audience gauges the quality of a talk by what they see and hear. Because they can't see you (unless you are using a webcam) what they hear becomes more important. Your voice needs to be more exciting in a virtual presentation. People are bored more easily in a virtual presentation so your voice has to be energizing (and if you can't do energizing, at least try to be more exciting). Energizing doesn't necessarily mean speak faster. There is a tendency with virtual presentations to talk fast because you can't see the audience. Don't be afraid to use dramatic pauses or pauses between slide transitions. Third, if you still can't control your "um's" between sentences, then you are in for a painful virtual presentation because "um's" are more obvious when people are focusing on your voice. Lastly, because virtual presentations are less interactive try to find different ways to engage the audience. This may include asking them questions and using the polling function of the presentation software or asking hypothetical questions. If you do a simulation, you might ask the audience "What do you think the results will be?" then use the chat function to get some answers. Most presentation software also have annotation tools that you can use during your presentation. Become familiar with the use of these and then use them during your talk to highlight things on a slide.

Concluding Remarks

The key to overcoming a fear of public speaking is public speaking. Speaking metaphorically, being well prepared helps open the door, but it's the actual act of speaking in front of others that allows you to walk through the door. Unfortunately, there are few opportunities for public speaking while in school. Teachers rarely assign oral presentations in class. As a result, students are simply not prepared for the speaking demands of a professional scientist after they graduate. It is only through the actual repeated act of giving a presentation, which is a kind of on-the-job-training, that people learn to become a more polished and accomplished speaker. I have found that over time as I became more and more comfortable speaking in front of a crowd I was able to focus more on what I wanted to say instead of focusing on how I will be feeling during a presentation. Hence, by becoming more comfortable in front of an audience you will learn to be able to focus more on the audience needs rather than your needs.

– Seven –
Questions, Criticisms, and Conflict

In the late 1990s Ed Yardeni at Deutsche Morgan Grenfell published a model to be used as a stock valuation tool that has since been called the "Fed's Stock Valuation Model," which is actually ironic since the Federal Reserve System ("the Fed") has never endorsed this model (Yardeni, 1997; Yardeni, 1999). It's a simple model that states that the inverse of price-to-earnings ratio (E/P) is in equilibrium with the 10-year bond yield of a Treasury note (Y10)

$$\frac{E}{P} = Y10 . \tag{4}$$

This relationship is shown in Figure 49. If you don't know what these terms mean, price-to-earnings (P/E) ratio is the ratio of the current stock share price to its annual earnings per share. A high P/E ratio shows high demand for a share of a company's stock and can be interpreted as the number of years of earnings required to pay back the stock purchase price.

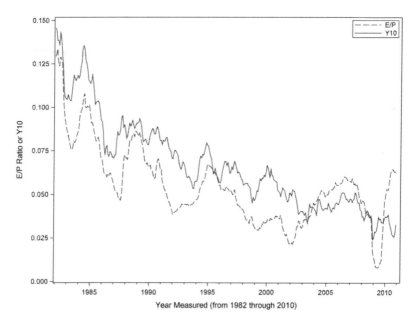

Figure 49. Standard & Poor's 500 E/P ratio (dashed line) versus 10-year Treasury bond yield (Y10, solid line) from 1982 to 2010. *Reference: http://www.multpl.com/table and http://research.stlouisfed.org /fred2/data /GS10.txt,, accessed 1 October, 2014.*

For example, Apple was trading at $532.17 at the end of 2012 and reported an earnings per share of $13.81. Hence, its P/E ratio was 38.5, which is considered quite high, and means it would take almost 40 years before your investment in 1 share of stock paid for itself. The Fed model doesn't use P/E ratio and instead uses its inverse, the E/P ratio. The 10-year bond yield is the interest rate the U.S. Treasury government pays for a bond that matures over 10 years, similar to the interest rate you pay when you borrow money on a loan. If you pay $1000 for a bond and over 10 years it returns $100, its yield is 10%.

Investors have a choice. They can invest in stocks or they can invest in bonds. The Fed model can be used to help one choose where to invest their money. If E/P and Y10 are out of alignment then one should invest in whatever will bring it back into alignment. If E/P > Y10 then stocks yield more than bonds, are more attractive than bonds as investments, and business pundits often say that stocks are "undervalued." If E/P < Y10 then bonds yield more than stocks, are more attractive than stocks, and stocks are "overvalued." For example, if E/P is 8% and Treasury note yield is 4%, then stocks are undervalued and it may be a good investment to shift money from bonds into stocks.

Despite its widespread use and acceptance (Thomas, 4-1-2008), the Fed model has been criticized every which way (Estrada, 2009). It has been criticized as being too empirical and lacking a theoretical foundation, that the model was built using only U.S. stock market data and for only a 15-year period from 1982 to 1997, i.e., the model was based on "carefully chosen and limited evidence," that the model does not apply to international markets, that the model no longer applies to today's markets, that using an equal sign is too strict (that at best the equality is approximate), that the model is misspecified, that the model violates statistical assumptions since it was based on regression-based methods and the data do not support a methodology, that the model breaks down when inflation and interest is low, and that the model has substantial deviations and is not predictive.

Suppose you are Ed Yardeni and you just presented your model to an audience. Afterwards, they are going to have questions. Was his model based on empiricism or mechanism? Was the relationship between E/P and Y10 something observed by chance or did it have some basis in theory? Did he test for any nonlinearities in the data? Why did he study only between 1982 and 1997? Did the model not work before 1982? Does it apply today? People always ask questions about models, ranging from some really stupid ones to ones that are quite challenging, and a modeler needs to know how to respond appropriately.

The first step to responding to questions is to stop talking and really, truly listen to the speaker. What is their question? What are they asking you? This may seem trivial and you may take listening for granted ("I listen all the time"), but listening to understand is a lot harder than it sounds because listening and hearing are not the same thing, especially when you are in front of an audience. You may be on a stage with hundreds of people looking at you or you may be in a small group where some senior manager is asking you questions. In either case you're going to be nervous. When we're questioned about our work, especially in front of an audience, it's natural for our sympathetic nervous system to release epinephrine into our bloodstream causing our heart rate to increase. Our skin becomes pale. We get tunnel vision making it difficult to internalize our surroundings and cortisol is released which can impair memory retrieval. This is the classic fight or flight response. In these circumstances, it's hard to listen. You have to push down all that emotion and listen. Focus on remaining cool and calm. Don't let the question freeze you. Table 2 presents some other tips on how to effectively listen.

It's important to remember that it's okay to not know the answer to a question. I think this may be one reason people don't like public speaking – that they may be asked a question that they don't know the answer to. If you don't know, you have options. You could redirect the question back to them and try to get more information which might help you get to an answer. You could direct the question to someone who helped developed the model and might be able to answer the question. If you just don't know, it's perfectly acceptable to say "I don't know." You could then add something like you will find out and get back to them with the answer. If you do say something like this, make sure you do indeed get back to them with the answer.

However you respond, don't be a jerk – be respectful of the other person, even if they are being a jerk. Let them get belligerent. Let them show the emotion. If one of you gets angry or acts like a jerk, most people will side with the other, respectful person and agree with them. Too much emotion in the workplace or at a conference never goes over well. If you have to get emotional, attack their argument, never attack them personally. Also, if the question is stupid (at least to you) then respond by simply answering the

---

Table 2

Ten Steps to Effective Listening

1. Face the speaker and maintain eye contact.
2. Be attentive, but relaxed.
3. Keep an open mind.
4. Listen to the words and try to picture what the speaker is saying.
5. Don't interrupt and don't impose your solutions.
6. Wait for the speaker to pause to ask clarifying questions.
7. Ask questions to ensure understanding.
8. Try to feel what the speaker is feeling.
9. Give the speaker feedback.
10. Pay attention to nonverbal cues – body language.

Reference: (Schilling, 11-9-2012).

---

question and don't mock them. This may seem obvious but you would be surprised how some people respond to stupid questions.

Make sure you understand the crux of their argument before your respond. If you don't understand the question, don't hesitate to get more information. Sometimes you may need to reflect or paraphrase the question back to the questioner to ensure you understand the question. Salespeople use the term "probing questions," which are detailed open-ended questions to get greater clarification and detail about some question or problem. Sample clarifying questions are:

- What did you mean by that?

- What, specifically, are you referring to?

- Tell me more about what you mean?

- I don't understand. Can you please clarify what you mean?

Sometimes what they said was vague and you need to prod them a little for more information:

- Can you be more specific?

- When you said "X," what were you referring to?

You could ask for examples:

- I don't understand. Can you give me an example?

- Are there any references I can use to look up what you are referring to?

- Have you tried such a model before?

The whole idea here is to respect the questioner and ask open-ended questions that do not presuppose an answer to get a further understanding of their question.

Everyone, before they even give their presentation, should have standard responses to common questions and model criticisms in their field. With regards to your model try to be prepared for common objections that can be raised. This way you are not caught off guard when people ask you a question or when your model is criticized. Here are some common questions/criticisms and some possible responses:

- "You just said you made assumptions about the model. What if your assumptions are wrong?" You could reply: "All models make assumptions. In this case the assumptions we made were relatively minor. Just to be sure we looked at how the results changed when we changed the model assumptions and found the results to be robust to the assumptions we made. So we are confident in the model and its predictions."

- "It's just a model." Everyone has a button that when pressed, pushes them over the edge. This is my button. When someone says

Figure 50. This is not an appropriate response to criticism. *Image courtesy of http://www.simpsoncrazy.com.*

this to me, I can imagine myself jumping over the table and yelling "So were Newton's laws of motion, you twit, but they got us to the !#$@* moon, didn't they!" as I am throttling them like Homer Simpson does to Bart (Figure 50). But of course this is not how I respond. After taking a moment to pause, I might reply "I agree. It is just a model and it may be imperfect. But without it, we have to use our gut to come to a decision. With it we have a rational basis, rightly or wrongly, on which to make a decision."

- "You have the wrong model", or if they think they are really clever they mangle George Box's famous quote, "All models are wrong." I would first try to determine what they mean. Can they be more specific? A generic response could be: "Models are neither right nor wrong. To say that a model is wrong is like saying a painting is pretty. It's all subjective. Physicists say $E=mc^2$ is wrong – it's too simplistic. Models are approximations. $E=mc^2$ is a really good approximation. The question is, 'How does this model perform? Does it answer the question we set out to solve?' Yes, it does. It's a good approximation to the system. It may not be 'right' but it's useful for what we need it to do."

199

- "Why didn't you develop a more mechanistic-based model?" You could reply "There weren't any advantages to developing a mechanism-based model but there were a whole host of disadvantages. Developing a mechanistic model would require us to make more structural assumptions about how the components interact in the model and would require us to estimate a large number of possibly unidentifiable parameters in order to use the model. Since we were simply interested in making predictions that don't require extrapolation, in this case, an empirical model seemed to be the best choice."

- "Your model is too complicated." First you should probe some more about what in particular they find objectionable about the model and then respond appropriately. A generic response might be something like "In a sense you're right. We did have to impose some complexity into the model but this was needed because of the dimensionality of the system. We did try to make sure that we weren't over-fitting the model through use of predefined model selection criteria."

- "The model is too simple." This criticism is usually code for the model is not mechanistic enough and that its assumptions are too simple to represent reality. A key question might be to reflect back to the questioner, "It is a simple model. But does it meet our needs? Is the model good enough right now? I think that it is."

- "There are too many assumptions in the model." This may be the most common criticism for mechanistic-based models. You need to think carefully about this one because there may indeed be a lot of assumptions in the model. One argument I have used was to ask, "What was the goal of the analysis?" If the goal of the analysis was to summarize the results of an experiment into a few model parameters then having a system with too many assumptions may be a valid criticism. However, if the goal of the model was to predict the results of an experiment using conditions outside the range of data used to build the model, then indeed a system with many assumptions may be needed because of the extrapolation. The other argument I sometimes make is that whatever analysis we do, whether it is analysis of variance (ANOVA) or mathematical modeling, models and assumptions are made. For instance, an ANOVA is based on a linear model with very specific assumptions, like normality and independence, regarding the distribution of residuals. The point being that all analyses make assumptions. The more assumptions you are willing to make, the more you can do with your model.

Not long ago, I witnessed an interesting situation for another modeler. I was in the audience of a national scientific meeting of modelers and other scientists from the pharmaceutical industry. The speaker was a modeler who was relatively new to the field and he was presenting the results of a model he developed. After he presented, a very-well known, out-spoken modeler questioned him about his results and specifically grilled him about models he could have tried but didn't. The obvious attitude of the well-known modeler was one of dismissal because he believed that the models that weren't examined were more appropriate or could have been better than the model that was presented.

This type of question is different from clarifying questions. With a clarifying question, the questioner wants more information and wants to learn something, but some questions are not really questions, they're criticisms. With criticism comes an emotional component between the criticizer and presenter that can be quite personal. That there may be another model not examined that is better than the one that was presented is a common model criticism. Most certainly there is. For any real world, complex problem there are a multitude of potential models, any one of which could be "better" than your model. Like miners during the Gold Rush always looking for gold around the next bend in the river, fellow modelers are ready and willing to offer advice on finding you a better model. "Did you try this model or that model?" they ask, always in the background the implication being that if you didn't try the model they suggested then the model you developed is somehow inferior or invalid.

Figure 51. The Rashomon effect, coined after a 1950 Japanese movie about the search for a killer in the Edo period, is when a multiplicity of models similarly "explain" a set of data. *Image reprinted from Wikimedia Commons.*

That a number of different models may explain the same set of data is called the Rashomon effect, which was first coined by Leo Breiman (2001). Rashomon was a movie made in 1950 by the Japanese director Akira Kirosawa. The story involves the death of a samurai in the Edo period of Japan in the city of Kyoto and the search to identify his killer. The story is told in courtroom testimony from the different points of view of the four participants in the event. All present the same set of facts, but the points of view are different, each equally plausible. The killer is finally revealed in the end. The theme of the movie is that there are many different viewpoints to an event, any one of which could be right. When applied to modeling, the Rashomon effect means that different models may each equally explain the same set of data. Each may be right and none may be right. Breiman gives an example of a linear regression problem with 30 variables with the goal of finding the best 5-variable model. There are 140,000 different combinations. If the models is chosen with the lowest residual sum of squares (RSS), then there is a high likelihood that there will be a multitude of models each having a RSS within 1% of each other, all of which perform equally well in terms of goodness of fit and prediction.

How should you respond to the criticism that there might be a "better" model out there that you never examined? First, you should decide whether the suggestion is valid. Maybe the questioner is right about the model they suggest. Maybe their model is indeed better than your model. That option should always be considered. If you still consider your model to be the best model and that it is unlikely another model will be a significant improvement over your model, there are many different ways to respond, always ensuring you reply calmly and rationally. You can try deflection: "No, that model was not explored. That is something certainly to consider and I will look into it when this meeting is over." You can try to minimize their comment: "Hundreds of different models were tried. This model was the best and it met all the criteria I set prior to model development." If the speaker is acting belligerent you can be a little more forceful when replying: "Hundreds of different models were tried. The likelihood of the model you are suggesting being a significant improvement over the model I just presented is small. Next question." Recognize however that the more forceful you respond, one of two things is likely to result: either they will back down or their belligerence will escalate.

As illustrated by all the criticisms of the Fed model, models are contentious. Most people don't understand them. They distrust them. They're skeptical of the results. They're hesitant to use them. It's your job to get the audience to believe in the model and its results. You start by getting them to believe in you. You do that by building trust and, when possible, using collaboration to make them feel that the model is theirs and that they own the model. Even after all this expect to be criticized for both the model and for its predictions. That is a fact. All models are criticized. A person may not accept the model itself, the assumptions to build the model, the data used to build the model, the process of building the model, or the results of the model. Every step of model building is subject to criticism. It's unavoidable so you need to learn how to deal with criticism and to resolve conflict when the critics cannot be satisfied.

For some people, criticism of their work is a personal attack. It's upsetting and can lead to anger and resentment. Seek to understand the source of the criticism and their reason for the criticism. Certainly there are people who criticize as a form of socially acceptable bullying. After all, they are not attacking you, they are questioning the model. However, in many instances, the criticism usually comes from a lack of understanding or from a genuine interest in the model and wanting to improve it.

Criticism does have some genuine advantages. Some may say that criticism is the basis of science. Criticism offers new perspectives and allows you to improve as a modeler. Personally, criticism allows you to practice active listening, teaches humility, and teaches coolness under pressure. Criticism forces you to think quickly and problem solve in an extremely short period of time while under duress. Criticism also allows you to teach and improve others views toward you. You can teach others about modeling while at the same time showing them your analytical skills and interpersonal skills. When answered to someone's satisfaction, it increases your credibility with others and your self-confidence making it easier to answer questions and address criticisms in the future.

When you respond, whatever you do, don't get angry and lash out or get defensive. Don't immediately prove the other person wrong or dismiss their comment. When we get angry our brain starts issuing "fight or flight" responses. Our respiration increases. Our judgment gets cloudy. It's difficult to focus on everything around us. Hence, the first thing that needs to be done whenever criticism is leveled at your model is to recognize your emotions and where you are at inside. Some people take criticism, even when it is not personal criticism, very harshly, maybe even as a personal attack on themselves. When that happens our amygdala starts to take over and hijacks the higher parts of our brain responsible for logical thought (Goleman, 1996). Have you ever been in an argument where you can't think straight? That's your amygdala, taking over from the neocortex, preventing you from forming logical thoughts. That same emotional response happens to some people when they are responding to comments and criticism of their models.

How do you stop this from happening? First, you need to accept that criticism is a fact of life and modeling has always had its critics. Second, recognize the situation. Your heart is beating faster, you can feel the stress, and you can feel the emotions starting to pour out of you. Once you realize this, take a few seconds to breathe. Now is not the time to lie to yourself and tell yourself that everything will be fine. It's okay to tell yourself, "Oh, crap. Here comes the criticism." When you admit to yourself that you know it's criticism and that you are scared then an emotional release will occur and the amygdala will relinquish control back to the neocortex. You can then start to recenter yourself and move from "Oh, crap" to "Oh, well." Refocus your energy and then move onto addressing their concerns.

Once you are in the "Oh, well" phase, begin to assess the validity of the questioner's comment. Look at the criticism from their point of view because whatever their concern is, they may very well be right. It is important to remember that even a bully may sometimes be right. Modelers and their models are like mother tigers and their cubs. Heaven help those that get between them. A modeler or a modeling team may have overlooked something. There may indeed be a better model out there that wasn't considered. There may have been something wrong in building the model or some critical violation of assumptions. The results may have been misinterpreted. The trick is to determine whether their comments and criticisms are legitimate and do they have a point?

Whatever the criticism the response should be dealt with using grace and aplomb. You don't have to respond to a question right away. Take a few seconds to collect your thoughts and respond. Start off in a friendly manner. It's always useful to thank the questioner without being defensive. You can reply something like "That's a good point." or if something wasn't considered you could say that you "hadn't thought of that." Acceptance of their criticism gives the questioner validation and makes them more likely to be positive about your response.

Look for common ground. If you can't agree on everything, find the things you can agree on. Agreeing on some things facilitates agreement on later things. Sometimes during the course of questioning the argument may resolve itself as the disagreement becomes more refined allowing you to address their concerns. One tactic for an especially difficult questioner is to allow the other person to talk, sometimes as much as possible, as they may wear themselves out during their argument. A useful paradigm is to listen, clarify, assess, then speak – repeat as needed.

Respond to their comment, coolly and calmly. Be in control. You are the expert. Don't be arrogant but be confident in your responses. Assess whether they have all the information. Did they misunderstand something? You might reflect the question back to them by saying something like "So as I understand your question, you want to know how the impact of neglecting a potential variable may affect our results?" If you can't respond calmly, you might simply state "Good point" or some other noncommittal response and then move on. Try to let the other person do most of the talking. If you are wrong, don't hide the fact. Acknowledge the mistake and discuss how the mistake will be rectified.

Some criticism is unfair. There may be personal reasons behind the question, maybe the person is having a tough time in their life and this is an opportunity to vent some frustration. Maybe a hidden agenda is involved. Maybe the model results have implications for some other group and they may be trying to discredit the model or even the modeler. Whatever the reason, these are tough questions to respond to. Sometimes the person doing the questioning is so blatantly biased that others see it for what it is. Other times the criticism is more subtle. The best you can do is again to reply coolly, rationally, treat their questions with respect, answer them to the best of your ability, and remember that you are not your work, you are not your model.

There are going to be times when no matter how much you try to reply, deflect, or answer their question directly some people are not going to accept your model nor are they going to accept your results and conclusions. At this point, interaction with the questioner may become contentious and even heated. Conflict arises and conflict resolution techniques are needed to resolve the impasse. Being able to resolve the impasse is important because sometimes unresolved issues can decrease your credibility and cloud the model's validity. Resolution of the impasse, however, leads to greater credibility for the model afterwards so it is important to resolve any suggestions that the model is inadequate or invalid. Further, by standing up to a difficult questioner, the modeler has stood up to the test and showed his mettle. People respect that. Resolution of the conflict can be useful because it could lead to greater awareness of the problem, increased understanding of the model, and better group cohesion. If the conflict is not resolved the credibility of the modeler can be damaged and can be damaging to group dynamics. Resentment may linger if the conflict turns angry. Some people don't like conflict and may mentally disengage from a team.

When there is an impasse, there are really only a few options (Raffel, 2008):

1. Give in and agree with them. This is obviously the simplest response, but it may not be the best for you in the long run.

2. Compromise. Agree with some of what they say. It's been said that the best compromises are those where neither side is happy.

3. Wait and see. Don't outright disagree with them. Agree that you will look into whatever their disagreement is and get back to them on what you find out.

4. Agree to disagree. When this happens, neither you nor the questioner can find common ground. You both tolerate the other side's argument but don't agree with them.

5. Don't agree and dig in. This option leads to an irreconcilable impasse from which neither side budges. Sometimes this is the only option if you are absolutely certain the other side is wrong but make sure you have the political clout and credibility to pull off such a maneuver.

6. Give up and walk away. While in impasses in your personal life this may be an option, in your work life this is not a solution. In your personal life you may be able to just get up and walk away from an argument but most times at work this is a non-option. Walking out of a meeting is a possibility but the long-term consequences can be disastrous.

There are many different schools of thought regarding conflict resolution. The different ways to approach conflict resolution tend to reflect the profession of the mediator. We are going to look at two of them: principled negotiation and humanism. The former, developed by lawyers, is based on the best-selling book *Getting to Yes* by Roger Fisher and William Ury (1991). The premise is to take the people and personalities out of the problem and to not argue over positions. Focus on interests. How do positions and interests differ? A position is what they want, while an interest is why they want it. Arguing over positions results in people getting entrenched in their position as their ego becomes more and more associated with the position. Arguing over positions causes people to lose sight of their interests and their underlying concerns. In effect, as people become entrenched by their position, they forget why they have that position in the first place. If you look at interests you might be able to find a solution that might not have been evident from their position. Also, positions tend to appear intractable as both sides want different things. They appear to be either yes or no; "yes I will agree with you" or "no I will not." Interests, on the other hand, may have many different solutions. Once you start focusing on interests you should try to generate different options that benefit both parties using an objective criteria to choose a solution.

Principled negotiation is based on a search for results and takes people out of the problem. Humanists, on the other hand, still search for results but consider the parties involved when searching for a solution. A central theme in the humanist approach is that people need to feel valuable during the negotiation process (Cloke and Goldsmith, 2011; Goulston, 2010; Raffel, 2008). Probably the best known humanist approach is the Thomas-Kilmann approach (Figure 52) which was proposed in 1974 by Kenneth W. Thomas and Ralph H. Kilmann, both of whom were psychologists. The Thomas-Kilmann Conflict Mode Instrument (1974) is a test designed to understand your "conflict style." How do you respond to conflict? Do you shrink from conflict or do you avoid it? Do you get angry? By understanding how you respond to conflict you can better prepare yourself for when conflict does arise.

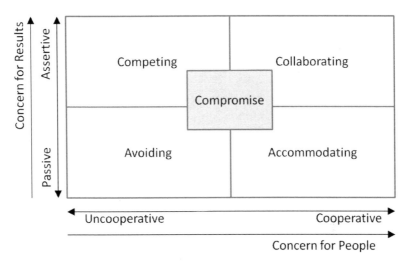

Figure 52. Thomas-Kilmann Conflict Mode Instrument measures a person's default style for conflict resolution.

After completing the test, of which there are a number of different versions (http://www.kilmanndiagnostics.com), the respondent is rated on two scales, concern for results and concern for people, and classified into one of five categories:

- **Competing**: high in assertiveness and low in cooperation. You neglect the concerns of others to satisfy your own concern using whatever it takes to win.

- **Avoiding**: low in assertiveness and cooperation. You tend to avoid conflicts by being uncooperative and passive.

- **Accommodating**: low in assertiveness and high in cooperation. This is the opposite of competing. You neglect your concerns for the concerns of others through self-sacrifice. Accommodators tend to see harmony as more important than getting their way in conflicts.

- **Collaborating**: high in both assertiveness and cooperation. You try to find a solution that satisfies both parties without accommodating.

- **Compromise**: intermediate to both assertiveness and cooperation. You are willing to sacrifice some of your concerns so that a partial solution is achieved. You look for the most expedient, mutually acceptable solution such that neither party is completely satisfied.

The idea is that once you know your default conflict style you become aware of it and may be able to modify it. For example, accommodators naturally give in to others and recognizing that you are an accommodator may allow you to not be so quick to stop arguing a point. Also, by understanding the different styles you may be able to adapt them when the situation is appropriate:

- Competing is useful when a quick solution is needed, when the other person is belligerent, when the other person is trying to take advantage of you, or when you know you are right and simply don't care how this will affect the other person or their relationship with you afterwards. Sometimes this latter option is not really an option.

- Avoiding is useful when you need to buy some time before the conflict can be resolved or as a way to dispose of the matter. Avoidance is generally a lose-lose situation and it should be avoided (pun intended).

- Accommodating is useful when you realize you might be wrong and need to correct the situation, when you realize that what the other person wants is more important than what you want and you are willing to accommodate them to gain good will, when you need to preserve harmony, or to build good will with the other person.

- Collaboration is the best of both worlds where both you and the other person's needs are met. Collaboration is where trust is built. It should be used whenever possible.

- Compromise is useful when you need a quick and easy solution to a problem, when two equally powerful individuals have mutually exclusive goals, or when other styles fail.

How you decide to respond should depend on what kind of relationship you want to have with that person later and what results you want to achieve (Cloke and Goldsmith, 2011). There will be times when you should back down, times when you should fight, and times when you should compromise. Principled negotiation is not right for all situations. In principled negotiation you are to take the other person out of the equation and focus on the interests. At work, you are most often in conflict with people you need to work with after the conflict is resolved. It's impossible to separate the people from the problem. Hence, a humanist approach may be better at work, but principled negotiation might be a useful approach at a conference with people that you might not deal with day after day.

If the impasse is with a superior, some people are not comfortable arguing with a superior and choose to give in and agree with them as the easiest course of action. This indeed may be the only option depending on the type of person the superior is. Arguing with a superior is never easy but paradoxically it has been reported that agreeably disagreeing with higher-ups increases the likelihood for promotions and advancement (Lublin, 8-9-2012). I need to point out here that there is a difference here between arguing and agreeably disagreeing. Arguing is belligerent and emotion is involved. Agreeably disagreeing is respectful and takes the personal component out of the equation. Differences of opinion do not have to lead to an argument. It's never easy to argue with a superior. It takes courage and that is seen as a positive thing. It's never good to use this approach when you are new to a company or position, but choosing which battles to fight, keeping cool, not treating the other person like an idiot, and using a compelling argument boosts your credibility.

Figure 53. If only Alexander Hamilton had known his conflict style, things might have turned out differently for him. *Image reprinted from Wikimedia Commons.*

Let's see how these schools of thought compare. Suppose you have just presented your stochastic model of beach erosion in Lake Michigan and your projections on how much sand the city of Chicago needs to buy in the next five years. These projections are needed to start the contract process and to lock in a price because year-to-year purchases of sand are too expensive and a five year purchase can result in significant savings. A hand raises from the audience and its Dr. Grumpy, a professor who wrote a scathing book criticizing the use of models in the environmental sciences and a notorious critic of mechanistic modeling in general. He stands up and says "Quantitative models predicting the outcome of natural processes on the surface of the earth don't work. No quantitative model can ever predict the reality of nature." This is his position. You can either agree with him or disagree; there is no middle ground here. So how do you respond to his comment?

You could reply using the techniques of either principled negotiation or humanism, or some blend of both. In principle negotiation, you need not consider who he is or what emotional baggage might be attached, but instead focus on the issues. His comment had no substance, nothing of any detail for you to reply to. To find out you could ask "Help me to understand why you think quantitative models offer no value?" He would probably reply that nature is too complex, that we don't have an understanding of all the variables that are in play, that we don't understand how they interact, and that even if we could understand all the variables at play, the uncertainty in their estimates would make the predictions worthless. Okay, so now we are getting somewhere. His concern, his interest, is that nature is too complex and that no quantitative model could ever account for that level of complexity. You might reply "I agree with you. No model ever perfectly represents reality for any problem. Help me to understand, what are you afraid might happen if we use the model?" He might reply "You could be seriously wrong in your estimate of the degree of beach erosion." You might then reply, "If I understand you correctly, you are concerned that since the model could never perfectly represent reality, its predictions might not be accurate. Is that correct?" He would reply "Yes," so then you could reply, "You make a strong case. What could I do to my model to make it acceptable to you?" At this point he will either start being supportive or will remain uncooperative. He might then reply "Nothing. Quantitative models aren't worth the paper they're written on." Clearly, he is not going to budge from his position. You might then reply "Okay, let me ask you, if you could have any solution to this problem, what might it be?" He may then reply "I would look at the trend in solid erosion over the last decade and extrapolate out to the next five years." So it might go back and forth discussing the merits of his proposal. It's doubtful that you would ever get Dr. Grumpy to agree to your model so the best you can hope for is to make him feel that his argument is understood because arguing with him is pointless.

On the other hand, a humanist might respond to his comment with "Thank you Doctor Grumpy. I can see that you feel passionately about this. Can you elaborate on your comment?" Grumpy might further elaborate on the near impossibility to adequately characterize the processes being modeled and that many processes are being omitted from the model. A humanist might then respond "Thanks. I can now see why you are pretty upset about this. I think you are right. No quantitative model of this type can account for all the factors involved. We did have to simplify the system and make some assumptions in order to make the problem solvable. Thank you for pointing that out to the audience. Let me ask you, if you were me, how would you go about modeling this data? Keep in mind that we need to be able to get projections of how much sand to buy in the next five years?" Notice the difference from the principled negotiation approach. The humanist approach is more touchy-feely and more open about feelings and validation of opinions. Grumpy might respond "I would look at the trend in solid erosion over the last decade and extrapolate out to the next five years." At this point you could argue the merits of his approach, i.e., take a competing approach and argue the merits of your model, or you could take a more collaborating/accommodating approach which might sound something like "That's a good point. What I like about what you said is that empirical models are certainly more flexible and easier to develop than mechanistic models. Why don't I go back to the office and do your model and see how the predictions compare with each other. Does that sound reasonable to you?" He might then reply "Yes." You could then reply "Good. So how would we decide which model is more appropriate?" You could then define some objective criteria from which to choose the most appropriate model and then move onto other questions.

These two scenarios were meant to illustrate the differences between the humanist and principled negotiation approaches, but you could also take a blended approach where principled negotiation is blended with humanist touches to make the questioner feel valued and that his opinions have merit. In the last scenario we agreed to explore the utility of his model and then choose the best option. Some might argue that we are capitulating and agreeing with him that our model is not useful. Quite the contrary, you both want the same thing - the best estimate of beach erosion over the next five years. It's simply a matter of how you get there. In this instance we examined our options and decided that it would be best to explore other options before making our recommendation.

In closing out this chapter, being able to answer questions and address comments, concerns, and criticisms with your models is part of a modeler's job. Sometimes it's just a matter of education. People simply don't understand the math or the concepts and it's your job to teach it to them. Sometimes however people may not like the model you developed for any number of reasons. That is why you must learn to maintain your composure. Relax. Don't let your amygdala take control and have you become an emotional volcano. Communication is one of the most important skills in life. You may not understand another person; they may not understand you. Actively listen and try to understand their issue. Ask probing questions when necessary. Pause if you need to collect your thoughts. When criticism turns into conflict, you have many choices in how you respond. Understanding your conflict style can help you in your choice. For example, if you are a natural accommodator, you can learn to be more collaborative or competing. You also have the option of what you say and how you say it. Whether you use principled negotiation or a humanist approach to reply to harsh criticism, don't melt under the pressure. Stay cool, be confident, and remember that this is your model. You know it better than anyone. You may not be able to resolve the impasse but standing up to the criticism is a good thing for both you and your model.

Seize Your Brand

Every time you walk into a room, every time you give a speech or a seminar, you are presenting yourself to others. When people see that you are speaking do they think "Oh, no, not that guy again?" or do they think "This will be interesting." When people see you at work, what do they think about you? Are you perceived as a subject matter expert? As happy or grumpy? Confident or insecure? Unflappable or nervous? Companies have brands, but so do people. Brands are what differentiate us from our competitors and the great companies spend a lot of effort to make sure their brand is known. Quick. What is Apple known for? It's innovation. How did you know that? By skilled and consistent branding by Apple. When applied to people, your reputation, how you are perceived by others, how you present, anything that differentiates you is your brand.

To start building your brand, ask yourself "What do I want people to think of when they think of me?" Are there general qualities you want people to associate with you like reliable or great communicator, or is there a particular area that you want people to know you are a subject-matter expert in? What things do you do better than others? What things don't you do well? What are you praised for by others? What excites you? What are you passionate about? Once you understand how you want to be perceived and how people perceive you right now, you can work to devise a strategy to meet those objectives. Dorie Clark has an excellent book called Reinventing You (2013) that can help you through this process. So take control of your brand.

– Eight –
Postscript

Professional athletes visualize themselves winning an event before it begins to improve their performance and gain a competitive edge. Let's apply this concept to our presentations. Before I begin please allow me to take some liberties and apply the visualization exercise to my field, the pharmaceutical industry. I think though that you will be able to see how this will apply to other fields.

Imagine you are at work. Your company is developing a new drug for the treatment of arthritis and the project team leader has selected you to identify the three doses, e.g., 25, 50, and 100 mg, that will be studied in a large-scale Phase 3 efficacy trial. You were chosen because you are a respected modeler who gets along well with others, is known to deliver projects on time, and has the skills necessary to solve the problem. In short, they trust you to solve the problem in a timely manner and the results you deliver will be believed.

So you put together a modeling group consisting of a programmer, statistician, pharmacokineticist, pharmacologist, and physician. You and the latter three scientists start to develop the conceptual mechanistic pharmacokinetic-pharmacodynamic (PKPD) model that will provide the relationship between dose and effect while you, the programmer, and the statistician start to identify the data available that can be used to build the conceptual model. The programmer develops the database that will be used in the analysis. As you start to develop the working model based on the conceptual model you meet regularly with the team to discuss roadblocks, places where the data might not support the model. Adjustments to the model are made. Assumptions that were made during development of the conceptual model are tested and those that are not supported are changed. A PKPD model is finally agreed upon by the modeling group and then together with the statistician and physician the model is translated to different clinical study designs with different doses, sample sizes, and clinical trial length. Together with the statistician, Monte Carlo simulation is used to identify the optimal experimental design and doses proposed for use in Phase 3. One important finding is that because of the variability across individuals and the shape of the dose-effect profile there is no advantage to using three doses in Phase 3. Studying two doses (e.g., 25 and 75 mg) has as much statistical power as studying three doses (e.g., 25, 50, and 100 mg) and will result in a cheaper clinical trial.

At the conclusion of the analysis, you are tasked to present the modeling group's results to the overall clinical development project team. This is to be an informal meeting. The audience consists of people of various backgrounds, but most of the technical people on the project team were part of the modeling group so the presentation needs to be kept simple. You start to think about your key message. What is it? It's not the model. The project team doesn't care about the model. The simulations are the key. With this in mind you start to prepare your slide deck focusing on the key message. You follow the five C's: consistent, clear, concise, cultured, and contents. The model is briefly presented in a high-level overview. No parameter estimates are shown. No goodness of fit plots are shown. The presentation focuses on the different simulation outcomes, how they were conducted, their results, and how they differ with regards to statistical power and clinical trial cost. You keep the presentation high-level and very pragmatic with regards to the outcome of the modeling exercise. Over the days prior to the presentation, you rehearse over and over what you are going to say, how you will say it, and the things you want to emphasize. In order to help facilitate the meeting on the day of the presentation, a few days before you meet with the project team leader to present your results so their questions and concerns are addressed beforehand.

On the day of the presentation you present to the project team the possible scenarios and the modeling group's recommendations for using two doses instead of three in the Phase 3 trials. You speak with confidence and exhibit trust-building behaviors with regard to body-language. You answer questions with authority. Things you don't know, you admit to, and agree to get back to the team on. There are no major concerns from the project team and in the end they agree with the modeling group's recommendations for doses. The analysis was a success and had a meaningful impact to the project.

Afterwards your boss asks to meet with you in a one-on-one to discuss the analysis. So you shift the focus of the presentation to your boss, the HIPPO. You know after observing your boss that they don't like a lot of details. They don't really want to know about the model other than a high-level overview. What they really want to know is how the work affected the project and what impact did you have on the project? They're a charismatic. So you rework your presentation, taking out a lot of the detail, instead focusing on high-level concepts like how your model captures the mechanism of action of the drug and how you were able to use Monte Carlo simulation to predict the doses to test in large scale clinical trials of efficacy and safety. Based on the simulations you were able to show that only two doses would need to be tested and that by using the two doses you suggest be used, instead of the three doses the project team leader wanted to use, you saved the company about 10 million dollars. This becomes your key message. Satisfied, your boss leaves happy and starts to spread the word about how valuable you and the department are to the company.

Later, you are invited to speak at a national meeting of theoretical biologists to present your model to them. So you shift the focus of your presentation again. This time your key message changes from the results of the model to the model itself. How was the model developed? What aspects of the biology were captured by the model? How did the mechanism of action translate to the clinical endpoint? These are the issues the audience is concerned with. You still follow the five C's but now you include slides on the model development process. You include slides on the initial model and show how the model was initially unidentifiable. Then you include slides on how you simplified the model and fixed parameters to literature values to make the model identifiable. You discuss your failed experiments treating the model as a Bayesian model with priors on some of the parameters but this did not improve the difficulty with identification of model parameters. You then move into the best model and discuss its advantages and limitations and how those limitations might affect decision making. You leave off entirely the results of the simulation.

On the day of the presentation, you're nervous but you don't show it. You've rehearsed this so many times you are confident of your success. You stand erect behind the podium, not leaning or swaying. You speak with authority. No "um's" or "uh's". You again exhibit trust-forming behaviors as you present. You know how to use the computer to change your slides. You know how to use the laser pointer. Afterwards, you are challenged by an audience member about the simplifications you made to the model to make the parameters identifiable. They are quite belligerent towards you but you respond coolly and calmly. You easily answer their question since you anticipated someone asking you this question and had come prepared with an answer. They continue to be quarrelsome having not been completely satisfied with your answer. You remain poised and ask to discuss this issue with them after the session to which they agree. With no other questions you sit down. Members of the audience that day remember your presentation and how you handled yourself with that jerk afterwards. You are remembered as an excellent speaker.

Over time you are seen as the go-to person for modeling and simulation at your company. You are viewed by others in your company as a strong modeler with excellent communication skills and are called upon by senior management to act as a translator to other modelers who are confusing and boring in their presentations. Outside your company you are seen as a great speaker who is frequently invited to give talks and make presentations. You may soon find that you, yourself, are not quite as nervous as you used to be. Presentations are easy for you now since you have mastered the skills needed to be a great model communicator.

References

Allen TJ. *Managing the Flow of Technology*. MIT Press, Cambridge, MA, 1977.

Allen TJ and Henn G. *The Organization and Architecture of Innovation: Managing the Flow of Technology*. Butterworth-Heinemann, Amsterdam, 2006.

Andrews P. Trust building for a virtual team. IBM Business Consulting Services; http://www-935.ibm.com/services/us/imc/pdf/g510-3949-trust-building.pdf; 2004, accessed 10-12-0014.

BBC News. A journey through Earth's climate history, 12-3-2009. (http://news.bbc.co.uk/2/hi/in_depth/sci_tech/2009/copenhagen/8393855.stm, accessed 10-1-2014).

Berkun S. There are two kinds of people: simplifiers and complexifiers. In: *Mindfire: Big Ideas for Curious Minds*, Berkun Media LLC, USA, pp. 33-34.

Birch SA, Akmal N, and Frampton KL. Two-year-olds are vigilant of others' non-verbal cues to credibility. *Development Science* 2010; 13: 363-369.

Breiman L. Statistical modeling: the two cultures. *Statistical Science* 2001; 16: 199-231.

Britton A and Shipley MJ. Bored to Death? *International Journal of Epidemiology* 2010; 39: 1-2.

Bumiller, E. We Have Met the Enemy and He Is PowerPoint. The New York Times, 4-26-2010. (http://www.nytimes.com/2010/04/27/world/27powerpoint.html, accessed 10-1-2014).

Chambers HE. *Effective Communication Skills For Scientific and Technical Professionals*. Perseus Publishing, Cambridge, MA, 2001.

Clark D. *Reinventing You: Define Your Brand, Imagine Your Future*. Harvard Business Review Press, Boston, MA, 2013.

Cleveland WS. *The Elements of Graphing Data*. Hobart Press, Summit, N.J., 1994.

Cloke K and Goldsmith J. *Resolving Conflicts at Work: Ten Strategies for Everyone on the Job*. Jossey-Bass, San Francisco, 2011.

Coppola NW, Hiltz SR, and Rotter NG. Building trust in virtual teams. *IEEE Transactions on Professional Communication* 2004; 47: 95-104.

Covey SMR. *The Speed of Trust: The One Thing That Changes Everything*. Free Press, New York, NY, 2006.

de Bono E. *The Six Thinking Hats: An Essential Approach to Business Management*. Little, Brown and Company, Boston, 1985.

DeSteno D, Breazeal C, Frank RH, Pizarro D, Baumann J, Dickens L, and Lee JJ. Detecting trustworthiness of novel partners in economic exchange. *Psychological Science* 2012; 23: 1549-1556.

Driver J. *You Say More Than You Think*. Crown Publishing Group, New York, 2010.

Duarte N. *Slide:ology: The Art and Science of Creating Great Presentations*. O'Reilly Media, Sebastian, CA, 2008.

Eigenbrode SD, O'Rourke M, Wulfhorst JD, Althoff DM, Goldberg CS, Merrill K, Morse W, Nielson-Pincus M, Stephens J, Winowiecki L, and Bosque-Perez NA. Employing philosophical dialogue in collaborative science. *Bioscience* 2007; 57: 55-64.

Embrechts P. Did a mathematical formula really blow up Wall Street? 2009 (http://www.actuaries.org/ASTIN/Colloquia/Helsinki/Presentations/Embrechts.pdf accessed 10-1-2014).

Estrada J. The Fed Model: the bad, the worse, and the ugly. *The Quarterly Review of Economics and Finance* 2009; 49: 214-238.

Fisher R, Ury W, and & for the second edition Bruce Patton. *Getting to Yes: Negotiating Agreement Without Giving In*. Penguin Books USA Inc., New York, 1991.

Flynn MR, Kasimov AR, Nave J-C, Rosales RR, and Seibold B. Self-sustained nonlinear waves in traffic flow. *Physical Review E* 2009; 79: 056113.

Gallo, F. Decision making in Chinese culture. CHO Magazine, (July and August) 2008.

References

Georges L and Guenzi P. Five trust building blocks; 2012 (http://www.provenmodels.com/548/five-trust-building-blocks/laurent-georges--paolo-guenzi/, accessed 10-1-2014).

Goleman D. *Emotional Intelligence: Why It Can Matter More than IQ*. Bantam Books, New York, NY, 1996.

Goulston M. *Just Listen: Discover the Secret to Getting Through to Absolutely Anyone*. American Management Association, New York, 2010.

Green C. Why trust is the new core of leadership; 4-3-2012 (http://www.forbes.com/sites/trustedadvisor/2012/04/03/why-trust-is-the-new-core-of-leadership/, accessed 10-1-2014).

Hansen MT. *Collaboration: How Leaders Avoid Traps, Create Unity, and Reap Big Results*. Harvard Business Press, Boston, MA, 2009.

Harrison S. *Idea Selling: Successfully Pitch Your Creative Ideas to Bosses, Clients, and Other Decision Makers*. HOW Books, Cincinnatti, OH, 2010.

Harrison-McKnight D and Chervany N. Reflections on an initial trust-building model. In: *Handbook of Trust Research*, (Ed. Bachmann R and Zaheer A). Edward Elgar Publishing Limited, Cheltenham, U.K., pp. 29-51.

Heath C and Heath D. *Made to Stick*. Random House, Inc., New York, NY, 2008.

Jones, S. The formula that felled Wall Street. Financial Times, 4-24-2009. (http://www.ft.com/intl/cms/s/0/912d85e8-2d75-11de-9eba-00144feabdc0.html#axzz2A4ZNnLJv, accessed 10-1-2014).

Kahneman D. *Thinking, Fast and Slow*. Farrar, Stratus, and Giroux, New York, NY, 2011.

Koegel TJ. *The Exceptional Presenter Goes Virtual*. Greenleaf Book Group Press, Austin, TX, 2010.

Krause A and O'Connell ME. *A Picture is Worth a Thousand Tables: Graphics in the Life Sciences*. Springer, New York, 2013.

LeFever L. *The Art of Explanation: Making Your Ideas, Products, and Services Easier to Understand*. John Wiley & Sons, Inc., Hoboken, NJ, 2013.

Lencioni P. *The Five Dysfunctions of a Team*. Jossey-Bass, San Francisco, CA, 2002.

Li D. On default correlation: a copula function approach. *Journal of Fixed Income* 2000; 9: 43-54.

Lloyd J. Presentation Disasters; 2014 (http://www.jobdig.com/articles /1883/Worst_Presentation_Disasters.html, accessed 8-12-2014).

Lublin, J. S. Arguing with the boss: a winning career strategy. Wall Street Journal, 8-9-2012. (http://online.wsj.com/article/SB10000872396390443991704 577579201122821724.html, accessed 10-1-2014).

Macfarlane AM and Ewing RC. *Uncertainty Underground: Yucca Mountain and the Nation's High-Level Nuclear Waste*. The MIT Press, Cambridge, MA, 2006.

Martinsons MG. Comparing the decision styles of American, Japanese, and Chinese Business Leaders; 2001 (http://papers.ssrn.com/sol3/papers.cfm ?abstract_id=952292, accessed 5-20-2013).

Mattessich PW, Murray-Close M, Monsey BR, and Wilder Research Center. *Collaboration: What Makes It Work*. Fieldstone Alliance, St. Paul, MN, 2001.

Maurer R. *Why Don't You Want What I Want? How to Win Support for Your Ideas Without Hard Sell, Manipulation, and Power Plays*. Bard Press, Atlanta, GA, 2002.

Mehrabian A and Ferris R. Inference of attitudes from nonverbal communication in two channels. *Journal of Consulting Psychology* 1967; 31: 248-252.

Miller RB and Williams GA. *The 5 Paths to Persuasion: The Art of Selling Your Message*. Time Warner Book Group, New York, 2004.

Misztal B. *Trust in Modern Societies: The Search for the Bases of Social Order*. Polity Press, Cambridge, MA, 1996.

Morris, E. Are you an optimist or a pessimist? New York Times Opinion Pages, 7-9-2012. (http://opinionator.blogs.nytimes.com/2012/07/09/are-you-an-optimist-or-a-pessimist/, accessed 10-1-2014).

Morris, E. Hear, all ye people; Hearken, O Earth. New York Times Opinion Pages, 8-8-2012. (http://opinionator.blogs.nytimes.com/2012/08/08/hear-all-ye-people-hearken-o-earth/?_r=1, accessed 10-1-2014).

References

National Public Radio. 20% Chance of Rain: Do You Need an Umbrella?; 7-22-2014 (http://www.npr.org/2014/07/22/332650051/there-s-a-20-percent-chance-of-rain-so-what-does-that-mean#polls, accessed 12-1-2014).

Paradi D. *Present So They Get It: Create and Deliver Effective Powerpoint Presentations Your Audience Will Understand.* self-published, 2012.

Phillips B. A better solution to "Do you have any questions?"; 2012 (http://www.mrmediatraining.com/2012/09/26/a-better-solution-to-do-you-have-any-questions-2/, accessed 10-1-2014).

Pilkey OH and Pilkey-Jarvis L. *Useless Arithmetic: Why Environmental Scientists Can't Predict The Future.* Columbia University Press, New York, 2007.

Raffel L. *I Hate Conflict: Seven Steps to Resolving Differences with Anyone in your Life.* McGraw-Hill, 2008.

Reimold P and Reimold C. *The Short Road to Great Presentations.* IEEE Press, Piscataway, NJ, 2003.

Roam D. *The Back of the Napkin: Solving Problems and Selling Ideas With Pictures.* The Penguin Group, New York, 2009.

Robbins NB. *Creating More Effective Graphs.* John Wiley & Sons, Inc., Hoboken,N.J., 2005.

Rodriguez-Brenes IA, Wodarz D, and Komarova NL. Stem cell control, oscillations, and tissue regeneration in spatial and non-spatial models. *Frontiers in Oncology: Molecular and Cellular Oncology* 2013; 3: Article 82.

Rossell R, Carcereny E, Gervais R, Vergnenegre A, Massuti B, Felip E, Palmero R, Garcia-Gomez R, Pallares C, Sanchez JM, Porta R, Cobo M, Garrido P, Longo F, Moran T, Insa A, De Marinis F, Corre R, Bover I, Illiano A, Dansin E, de Castro J, Milella M, Reguart N, and Altavilla G. Erlotinib versus standard chemotherapy as first-line treatment for European patients with advanced EGFR mutation-positive non-small-cell lung cancer (EURTAC): a multicentre, open-label, randomised phase 3 trial. *The Lancet Oncology* 2012; 13: 239-246.

Salmon F. Recipe for disaster: the formula that killed Wall Street; 2009 (http://www.wired.com/techbiz/it/magazine/17-03/wp_quant, accessed 10-1-2014).

Sanders T. *The Likeability Factor: How to Boost Your L-Factor and Achieve Your Life's Dream.* Three Rivers Press, New York, 2006.

Schilling, D. 10 Steps to effective listening. Forbes Woman, 11-9-2012. (http://www.forbes.com/sites/womensmedia/2012/11/09/10-steps-to-effective-listening/, accessed 10-1-2014).

Schurr PH and Ozanne JL. Influences on exchange processes: buyers' preconceptions of a seller's worthiness and bargaining toughness. *The Journal of Consumer Research* 1985; 11: 939-953.

Steel J. *Perfect Pitch.* John Wiley & Sons, Inc., Hoboken, NJ, 2007.

Stewart, I. The mathematical equation that caused banks to crash. The Guardian/The Observer, 2-11-2012. (http://www.guardian.co.uk/science/2012/feb/12/black-scholes-equation-credit-crunch, accessed 10-1-2014).

Straus D. *How to Make Collaboration Work.* Berrett-Koehler Publishers Inc., San Francisco, CA, 2002.

Sweller J. Cognitive load during problem solving: effects of learning. *Cognitive Science* 1988; 12: 257-285.

The Majority Staff of the Senate Committee on Environment and Public Works. Yucca Mountain: the most studied real estate on the planet; 3-1-2006 (http://epw.senate.gov/repwhitepapers/YuccaMountainEPWReport.pdf, accessed 10-1-2014).

Thomas J. Don't fight the Fed model!; 4-1-2008 (http://faculty.som.yale.edu/jakethomas/papers/fedmodel.pdf, accessed 10-1-2014).

Thomas KW and Kilmann RH. *Thomas-Kilmann Conflict Mode Instrument.* Xicom, a subsidiary of CPP, Inc., Mountain View, CA, 1974.

Tuckman B. Developmental sequence in small groups. *Psychological Bulletin* 1965; 63: 384-399.

Tufte ER. *Visual Explanations: Images and Quantities, Evidence, and Narrative.* Graphics Press, Cheshire, CT, 1997.

Tufte ER. *The Visual Display of Quantitative Information.* Graphics Press, Cheshire, CT, 2001.

References

Tufte ER. Powerpoint does rocket science - and better techniques for technical reports; 2011 (http://www.edwardtufte.com/bboard/q-and-a-fetch-msg?msg_id=0001yB, accessed 10-1-2014).

Vass J. *Soft Selling in a Hard World: Plain Talk on the Art of Persuasion.* Running Press, Philadelphia, 1998.

Whitehouse, M. Slices of risk. Wall Street Journal, 9-12-2005. (http://math.bu.edu/people/murad/MarkWhitehouseSlicesofRisk.txt, accessed 10-1-2014).

Williams GA and Miller RB. Change the way you persuade. *Harvard Business Review* 2002; 80: 65-73.

Wong DM. *The Wall Street Journal Guide to Information Graphics.* W.W. Norton & Company, New York, 2010.

Yardeni E. Fed's stock market model finds undervaluation. U.S. Equity Research, Deutsche Morgan Grenfill; 1997, accessed

Yardeni E. New, improved stock valuation model. U.S. Equity, Deutsche Morgan Grenfell; 1999, accessed

Zak PJ. The neurobiology of trust. *Scientific American* 2008; 298: 88-92.

Index

Index

About the Author

Peter Bonate has over 20 years experience in the pharmaceutical industry. He is currently Global Head of Pharmacokinetics, Modeling, and Simulation at Astellas Pharma. He has worked at GlaxoSmithKline, Genzyme, ILEX Oncology, Quintiles, Hoechst Marion Roussel, and Eli Lilly & Co. He received his PhD from Indiana University in Medical Neurobiology. He also received an MS in statistics from the University of Idaho and an MS in Pharmacology from Washington State University. He is a Fellow of the American College of Clinical Pharmacology and American Association of Pharmaceutical Scientists. He has served or currently serves on the editorial boards for the Journal of Clinical Pharmacology, Pharmaceutical Research, and the AAPS Journal and is the Associate Editor of the Journal of Pharmacokinetics and Pharmacodynamics. He is a frequently invited speaker at conferences and universities, has more than 50 publications in the field of pharmacokinetics and clinical pharmacology, is the co-editor of the three-volume series "Pharmacokinetics in Drug Development," and is author of the leading textbook "Pharmacokinetic-Pharmacodynamic Modeling and Simulation," currently in its second edition.

Made in the USA
Middletown, DE
04 December 2022

17028353R00137